Austrian Theory of Capital and Business Cycle

Pavel Potuzak

Austrian Theory of Capital and Business Cycle

A Modern Approach

palgrave
macmillan

Pavel Potuzak
Prague University of Economics and Business
Prague, Czech Republic

ISBN 978-3-031-18727-8 ISBN 978-3-031-18728-5 (eBook)
https://doi.org/10.1007/978-3-031-18728-5

This Palgrave Macmillan imprint is published by the registered company Springer Nature Switzerland AG.
The registered company address is: Gewerbestrasse 11, 6330 Cham, Switzerland

Acknowledgements

I am very grateful to the Prague University of Economics and Business and to my family for their long-term support. Without their help, this book would never have been realized and my entire research programme would be a complete misallocation of resources. The research in this book was supported by the grant of Prague University of Economics and Business VSE IGS F5/20/2022.

Contents

About the Author

Pavel Potuzak, Ph.D. lectures advanced macroeconomics, microeconomics, and Austrian economics at the Prague University of Economics and Business. His main fields of interest include theories of interest and capital, Austrian business cycle theory, and monetary economics. He has published several articles on these topics and has presented his research at international conferences, including ESHET, the Madrid Conference on Austrian Economics, and others. Potuzak is a founding member of the Institute of Economic Education (INEV), which organizes the Economics Olympiad for high school students in the Czech Republic and Central Europe.

List of Figures

CHAPTER 1

Introduction

This book is the result of my research into business cycle theory and the theory of capital over the last two decades. At the beginning of my investigations, I was positively impressed by the classical ideas of Friedrich August von Hayek. His insights were appealing and intellectually challenging, and seem to be confirmed by the performance of real-world economies. The financial crisis of 2007–2008 and the subsequent Great Recession reinforced my impression. These two events seemed to fit perfectly into Hayek's theory that economic depressions can occur even after periods of relative price stability and decent economic growth.

Austrian theory explains why seemingly smooth economic development can be interrupted by a sudden deterioration in economic conditions, even when there were no prior signs that the economy was heading down an unsustainable path. According to Hayek, the roots of business cycles should be sought in the banking and monetary system, in which the link between the acts of saving and investment is separated into two independent operations. Although money is one of the greatest inventions of human race, it also plays the role of a "loose joint" in markets, which can lead to serious imbalances between the demand for goods and the supply of goods, both within a given time period and between periods.

This process cannot be well understood without deep investigations of intertemporal markets and of the incentives of consumers and firms in these markets. One of the key findings of my research is that discrepancies in intertemporal markets can be exposed after a considerable period of

P. Potuzak, *Austrian Theory of Capital and Business Cycle*,
https://doi.org/10.1007/978-3-031-18728-5_1

time, when it is too late to respond in such a way as to restore the conditions of the intertemporal equilibrium that ruled before monetary disturbances began.

The scope of this research proved to be very broad. A proper understanding of intertemporal exchange required a thorough study of the theories of interest and capital to draw an accurate picture of the complex production processes in modern economies. In addition, because the major source of economic fluctuations has been identified in the monetary system, long-term research investigated not only authors writing in the Austrian tradition, but also modern monetary theorists, who revealed fascinating phenomena that were hidden from the eyes of the glorious scholars of the pre-war era.

The main outcome of this research is a new graphical apparatus that elucidates the core of Austrian capital theory. The same apparatus is also used in this book to describe Austrian business cycle theory, in which misallocation of resources in the production structure plays a central role.

The Austrian theory of capital emphasizes the time element in the production process. It differs from neoclassical theory, in which capital is considered a homogeneous mass. Austrian capital theory was designed to explain allocation of material resources that can change not only in the neoclassical long run, but also in the short run. The basic concept of capital in neoclassical theory, fixed capital, is not central to Austrian theory, because it lacks the key characteristics of capital from the Austrian perspective.

Chapter 2 of this book presents the main ideas of the founder of Austrian capital theory, Eugen von Böhm-Bawerk, in some detail. Emphasis is placed on the structure of production and the concept of roundaboutness. A new graphical model in this book clarifies misunderstandings that have appeared in the literature, especially those related to the higher productivity of roundabout methods.

Chapter 3 introduces a modelling tool developed by Friedrich August von Hayek, which is used to describe capital structure. At its heart is a discussion with Frank Knight and his idea that capital represents a homogenous mass that is automatically maintained. The Austrian model shows that capital has its own structure that cannot be ignored, and that the maintenance of capital is not automatic.

Chapter 4 presents five simultaneous short production methods that provide consumption goods in one period. A shock to time preference then triggers a gradual restructuring of the production apparatus. A new graphical model developed in this book shows how production processes are transformed into longer methods. The typical U-shaped dynamics of the flow of consumption goods is generated, and new capital goods are created that take the form of intermediate products. The reallocation of the labour force across specific labour markets is examined in detail, together with changes in the discounted marginal value product of labour in these markets.

The last part of Chap. 4 discusses the possibility of perpetual growth caused by a decrease in time preference, as predicted by some Austrian economists. The graphical model from the previous section is supported and compared with advanced neoclassical growth models to shed light on this issue.

Chapter 5 introduces Austrian business cycle theory. Business cycles seem to be a natural element of modern market economies. In the 1920s and 1930s, Friedrich August von Hayek developed a unique theory that identifies economic fluctuations with a deviation of the market interest rate from its natural level, leading to misallocation of resources in the production structure.

The same graphical model applied to capital theory examines the lengthening of production processes initiated by a monetary shock. The resulting dynamics of the economy resemble the paths set up by a fall in time preference. However, the model shows that some processes cannot be completed and will be abandoned. The graphical model explores the phenomenon of forced saving at the peak of the economic boom, and the partial destruction of capital in the downturn phase of the cycle.

Chapter 6 focuses on the dynamics of the interest rate over the business cycle predicted by Austrian theory. It primarily investigates the transmission mechanism that leads to a deviation of the market interest rate from its natural level and subsequent U-shaped behaviour of the market interest rate. Specific approaches by Hayek, Mises, and Rothbard are discussed in detail. This chapter also corrects misunderstandings and inconsistencies pointed out by critics of Austrian theory. The evolution of the interest rate in Austrian business cycle theory is then compared with the predictions of mainstream economics models.

The last section of Chap. 6 relaxes the assumption of a one-round increase in the money supply and describes continuous monetary expansion in detail. The analysis reveals that the market interest rate cannot be permanently reduced below its natural level. This section also explores the main forces that tend to raise the market interest rate.

Hayek admitted that the initial impulse that spurs a business cycle can arise in the real economy. Chapter 7 analyses a positive technological shock that leads to greater demand for credit, which is consequently accommodated by the banking system. The pattern of the Austrian business cycle is presented in the model developed in the previous sections. Although the emphasis is on the elastic money supply and its endogenous character, this section also introduces unstable demand for money as a possible source of economic fluctuations.

The core Austrian model implicitly assumes that the economy initially operates at its potential (natural) level of output. Chapter 8 relaxes this assumption. The consequences of monetary expansion are analysed in an economy with unemployed resources. This chapter shows that a business cycle can negatively affect potential output in the long run, due to misallocation of capital and its subsequent partial destruction. Chapter 8 also discusses the reasons for instability of the natural rate of interest over the business cycle. Austrian theory predicts that money may not be neutral even in the long run. Attempts by the central bank to follow the natural levels of economic variables can be futile, if the source of instability in the natural rate of interest and potential output is monetary policy itself.

It should be emphasized that Austrian theory has never been developed into a rigorous mathematical model. For this reason, this book applies textual arguments and graphs. Figures and numerical examples are introduced to guide sound reasoning, because one can easily become trapped in vicious circles when analysing a complex phenomenon such as the business cycle.

PART I

The Austrian Theory of Capital

CHAPTER 2

The Austrian Theory of Capital: A Basic Model

The Austrian theory of capital was outlined by Menger ([1871] 2007), thoroughly developed by Böhm-Bawerk ([1884] 1890, [1888] 1891), and refined by Hayek (1941) and Lachmann ([1956] 1978). The first problem encountered in investigation of this field is that various Austrian authors defined capital differently. Böhm-Bawerk (1890, p. 6) defined capital in his magnum opus as "a complex of produced means of acquisition". Hayek (1941, p. 9) partly diverted from this concept and stressed that capital is composed of non-permanent resources either produced by man or given by nature. Rothbard ([1962] 2004, p. 497) narrowed this definition and included only non-permanent produced means of production, whereas for Lachmann (1978, p. 11), capital was the stock of all material resources, including land. [1]

[1] Lachmann roughly accepted Irving Fisher's approach. For Fisher (1930), capital (or capital value) was just discounted future income, the source of which could be any wealth (including human beings). Lewin and Cachanosky (2019, 2021) defined capital in value rather than in physical terms, citing Mises ([1949] 1996) in this connection. However, they acknowledged that other Austrian authors emphasized the physical dimension of capital. See also Lewin (1999). Endres (1991, p. 70) argued that Wieser's definition of capital was similar to Hayek's. Endres also pointed out that Wieser's theory of capital was closer to Menger's than to Böhm-Bawerk's. Differences between Menger and Böhm-Bawerk are elucidated in more detail in Endres (1997, 167 ff.).

P. Potuzak, *Austrian Theory of Capital and Business Cycle*,
https://doi.org/10.1007/978-3-031-18728-5_2

Although many approaches to the definition of capital can be found, all Austrian authors stress that in the realm of capital theory, the crucial role is played by time. Capital goods are intermediary products on a time-consuming path to becoming final consumption goods (Böhm-Bawerk, 1890, p. 22). Almost no consumption good is created directly by labour and land. Instead of using labour and natural powers to make the goods prepared for immediate consumption directly, man undertakes an indirect route, a long roundabout journey, by creating intermediate products—capital goods—as shown not only by Böhm-Bawerk (1891), but by many authors before him, as Böhm-Bawerk (1890) himself demonstrated in his critique of the theories of his predecessors.[2]

Capital goods are productive in the sense that they create consumption goods—the only goods that, by definition, can satisfy human wants. Although the formation of capital goods precedes the creation of consumption goods in time, the value of capital goods is derived from the value of consumption goods. Capital goods acquire a value because consumption goods satisfy human wants. Once a capital good loses its power to create useful consumption goods, it becomes worthless. This can happen if the consumption good loses its value to the consumer, or if the capital good ceases to be used in the production of consumption goods.

This premise was applied not only by Menger (2007, p. 150) and Böhm-Bawerk (1890, 1891) to demolish old cost-of-production theories of value held by classical economists, but it was also stressed by Fisher (1930) in developing his own theory of interest. Although capital goods derive their value from consumption goods, after criticizing other authors and their theories in great detail, Böhm-Bawerk (1890, 1891) devoted almost one thousand pages to identifying and explaining the fact that one can always observe a difference between the value of capital goods and the final value of the consumption goods they eventually produce. This

[2] It may be interesting to add the definition of capital offered by William S. Jevons. Curiously enough, Jevons ([1871] 1957, p. 223) defined capital as "commodities which are required for sustaining labourers of any kind or class engaged in work". In this connection, he even added: "The capital is not the railway, but the food of those who made the railway" (Jevons, 1957, p. 243). Böhm-Bawerk (1890, p. 57) rejected this approach to capital, saying that a primitive tribe endowed with free food given by nature would then be the most capitalist nation in the world. However, another Austrian theorist, Strigl ([1934] 2000), partly adopted the Jevonian approach, stressing the significance of a subsistence fund in roundabout methods, detracting from the role played by particular capital goods.

positive premium or agio, as Böhm-Bawerk called it, is always present in the economy, and it is never eliminated by competition between entrepreneurs.

Two of the aforementioned elements are needed to explain this agio. The first is the fact that consumption goods are manufactured by capital goods, and capital goods derive value from consumption goods. The second is based on the observation that this indirect process proceeds in time. In other words, present capital goods will mature into consumption goods in the future. They are future consumption goods.

Böhm-Bawerk's solution is then condensed into a simple statement:

> *PRESENT goods are, as a rule, worth more than future goods of like kind and number. This proposition is the kernel and centre of the interest theory which I have to present.*
>
> Böhm-Bawerk (1891, p. 248)

If people value present goods more than future goods, then present capital goods, which will become future consumption goods, should be valued less than present consumption goods. Competition never eliminates this value difference. This statement plays a crucial role in explaining the positive interest rate in the economy. For Böhm-Bawerk (1891, p. 299), it provides a fundamental ground for the existence of natural interest on capital. Interest exists because people value present goods more than future goods. In other words, people are willing to exchange more future goods to obtain a lesser amount of present goods. They will sacrifice present goods only in exchange for a larger amount of future goods.

This theory can explain the existence of interest on loans. In a loan contract, people usually exchange money they presently hold for a greater amount of future money. The separation of principal and interest is only made for commercial and practical convenience (Böhm-Bawerk, 1891, p. 296). Interest is thus a widespread phenomenon, the importance of which should not be underestimated. Interest is immediately visible in the loan market. However, it is also pervasive in the production process, where it is expressed as a value difference between present consumption goods and present factors of production (capital goods), that is, as a value difference between present consumption goods and future consumption goods.

Böhm-Bawerk presented three grounds for the existence of interest. The first reason for the value advantage of present goods is that people are usually better supplied with goods in the future than in the present

(Böhm-Bawerk, 1891, 249 ff).[3] According to the marginal utility theory co-discovered by Menger ([1871] 2007), and further developed by Böhm-Bawerk (1891), an additional present consumption good thus provides greater marginal utility than a future consumption good. In essence, the last unit of a present good can satisfy more pressing needs than the last unit of a future good, because mankind will be supplied with more goods in the future. As a result, a marginal present good is valued more than a future good of the same type and quality.

Böhm-Bawerk (1891, pp. 250-252) further developed this idea. In reality, it can happen that the present is better supplied than the future. In this case, present goods can be stored and moved to the future. Due to the irreversibility of time (Hayek, 1941, p. 345), such a transfer can never be made with future goods, which provides an advantage to present goods. In addition, a new, initially unexpected need can arise between the moment the present goods are stored and the time the future goods become available. This need can be satisfied only with the present good. However, this argument only applies to goods that are easy to store. Goods that spoil rapidly over time are less likely to acquire this advantage.

The second reason for the agio between present and future goods lies in people's inclination to systematically underestimate their future wants (Böhm-Bawerk, 1891, p. 253). Fetter ([1915] 1928, p. 239), author of the term "time preference", emphasized that the act of valuing, whether present goods or future goods, always takes place in the present. Future valuation of future goods is not possible. Aware of this phenomenon even before Fetter, Böhm-Bawerk stated that in the present people underestimate future needs for the following three reasons.

The first is a built-in incomplete imagination of their future wants. The second is associated with a defect of the will, which leads people to prefer present satisfaction even at the expense of future inconvenience. The third arises from the uncertainty of the future, because one cannot know whether gratification from future goods will indeed materialize (Böhm-Bawerk, 1891, pp. 254-255).[4]

[3] This is true in a growing economy and on an individual level for most people during their pre-retirement lives. However, it seems to be much less tenable in a stationary economy.

[4] Similar ideas can be found in Jevons (1957), who described a lesser intensity of future anticipated feelings (1957, pp. 34-35) and the fact that future utilities must be weighed (i.e. scaled down) by the probability of their realization (1957, p. 72).

According to Böhm-Bawerk, undervaluation of future needs plays a role regardless of the relative provision of goods between the present and the future. In contrast to the first reason, a preference for present satisfaction should also apply in a stationary economy, in which the supply of goods is constant over time, therefore possibly constituting a stronger basis for the existence of a positive interest rate.

However, this explanation not only has been questioned by critics of the Austrian capital theory, such as Knight (1936), but has also been challenged by economists from within the Austrian school. Mises ([1949] 1996, p. 486), for example, rejected Böhm-Bawerk's reasoning on the grounds that the general characteristic of human action cannot be based on psychology. Mises elaborated on the original Böhm-Bawerk approach, stating that: "[s]atisfaction of a want in the nearer future is, other things being equal, preferred to that in the farther distant future" (Mises, 1996, p. 483).[5]

According to Mises, the preference for satisfying a given want in the present rather than in the future is a general feature of human action. After all, gratification of basic needs in the present is a necessary condition for survival in the future (Fetter, 1928, p. 241). Yet, Mises (1996, p. 487) emphasized that it is in effect not only in the extreme situation of preserving human life, but it is present in every choice people make.[6]

The first two reasons suggested by Böhm-Bawerk for the existence of a positive premium on present goods over future goods reveal that interest is a value phenomenon. They can be crucial for plotting an upward-sloping saving curve in the market for loanable funds. The subjective value premium on present goods is also closely related to a phenomenon which Fetter (1928, p. 236) termed time preference and which Fisher (1930) called impatience.[7]

[5] Traces of this idea can also be found in Menger (2007, p. 154): "*Setting aside the irregularities of economic activity, we can conclude that economizing men generally endeavor to ensure the satisfaction of needs of the immediate future first, and that only after this has been done, do they attempt to ensure the satisfaction of needs of more distant periods, in accordance with their remoteness in time.*"

[6] Potuzak (2016a, 2016b, 2016c) discusses whether this reasoning is strong enough to guarantee the existence of a positive natural (or originary) rate of interest under all circumstances, as postulated by both Mises (1996) and Rothbard (2004) and other proponents of the pure time preference theory.

[7] Fisher (1930) used the term "impatience" rather than time preference, arguing that it seemed less ambiguous. According to Fisher, time preference could also mean a preference for future goods over present goods.

The third reason put forward by Böhm-Bawerk introduced a technical or productivity element into his theory. According to Böhm-Bawerk (1891, p. 260), present goods are technically superior to future goods. This idea is based on several observations. The first is that when factors of production are employed in time-consuming roundabout methods, instead of being used directly in the production of final consumption goods, as a rule they are more productive in that they provide greater output of consumption goods.

This fact alone cannot give present goods any technical superiority. Locking present consumption goods in stock for some time will not wave a magic wand and increase the future output of consumption goods. The more correct reasoning lies in the fact that one can gain an advantage by controlling present consumption goods, as opposed to holding the same amount of future consumption goods. Factors of production can then be released from the processes that provide consumption goods directly or in a very short time, and applied to roundabout processes that take longer, but provide a greater output of consumption goods when completed. If people prefer a larger quantity to a smaller quantity of goods, a given amount of present goods must be valued more than the same amount of future consumption goods, because the present goods may eventually provide a greater output of future goods.

The idea of a roundabout production process lies at the centre of the Austrian theory of capital. During this process, capital goods of various forms are created by investing labour, land (or other types of natural resources), and other capital goods. Creation of intermediate products (capital goods) is not carried out for its own purpose. People undertake the time-consuming production process only because they believe that roundabout methods will provide a greater output of consumption goods.

It is surprising that Böhm-Bawerk never offered a reason why roundabout processes should have higher technical productivity than shorter methods that produce consumption goods directly using labour and land. On this point, Böhm-Bawerk merely stated:

> *That roundabout methods lead to greater results than direct methods is one of the most important and fundamental propositions in the whole theory of production. It must be emphatically stated that the only basis of this proposition is the experience of practical life. Economic theory does not and cannot show a priori that it must be so; but the unanimous experience of all the technique of*

production says that it is so. And this is sufficient; all the more that the facts of experience which tell us this are commonplace and familiar to everybody. But why is it so? The economist might quite well decline to answer this question. For the fact that a greater product is obtained by methods of production that begin far back is essentially a purely technical fact, and to explain questions of technique does not fall within the economist's sphere.

Böhm-Bawerk (1891, p. 20)

It was Hayek (1941) who later listed various reasons for the higher technical productivity of roundabout methods, although some traces of the most relevant explanations can also be found in Böhm-Bawerk (1891, p. 82) and Menger (2007, p. 73, p. 154). Roundabout processes usually employ resources that are not used or cannot be used in shorter processes that produce consumption goods directly (Hayek, 1941, p. 60). These were free (natural) resources that could only be applied if they were combined with other factors of production using methods that take much more time.

Taking time into account is again essential in this case. When people allocate their labour and land to the direct production of consumption goods, they do not have enough additional time available to employ unused natural resources. Even the proverbial Robinson Crusoe, who applied roundabout methods by creating a boat and a net, exploited materials that were not used to fish with one's bare hands. By engaging in roundabout processes, previously free non-economic goods may become scarce and ultimately no longer free. However, these goods would never become economic if other factors of production were not employed in roundabout methods of production (Hayek, 1941, p. 63).

The simple example of Robinson Crusoe can be extended to any degree. By additional lengthening of the production process, new resources that had been idle can be utilized to expand future output. As a result, roundabout methods are more productive simply because they exploit more natural resources and more natural powers that cannot be used with shorter methods due to lack of time. As Böhm-Bawerk (1891, p. 82) put it: "[N]ew allies are obtained from the immense stores of natural powers, and their activity is enlisted in the work of production".

Hayek (1941, p. 63) attributed the second reason for the greater productivity of roundabout methods to what he called the vertical division of labour.[8] In the longer methods, the production process can be separated into many sequential activities. This specialization makes the final product larger (or better serving, or satisfying more pressing needs) compared to shorter processes, for which the division of labour cannot be significantly extended. This reasoning therefore builds on the famous argument of Adam Smith ([1776] 1993).

The arguments usually put forward in favour of a horizontal division of labour, where people specialize in the production of various final consumption goods, can be used to support the argument of a vertical division of labour, in which activities are devoted to sequential production that is extended over time.[9]

The idea that roundabout methods are more productive is sometimes confusing. Since this piece of the mosaic of Austrian capital theory is widely used in Austrian business cycle theory, it should be clarified in detail. First, the idea is based on a generally accepted assumption of efficiency. If there are more methods of equal length that can produce the same consumption good, only the one that provides the largest output will be selected (Hayek, 1941, p. 73).[10] As a result, to achieve a larger output of consumption goods, factors of production must be employed in longer processes.

However, there is no guarantee that lengthening the process will result in greater production of consumption goods. The assumption of efficiency must again hold. Only the process with the largest output will be selected from a set of methods with a given (and now longer) period of production. In this case, the Austrian authors usually recall the Böhm-Bawerk (1891, p. 82) statement on "wisely chosen" roundabout methods.

It can also happen that the roundabout method (and the word "roundabout" is especially important here) produces the output in less time than the direct method.[11] The direct method is then out of the question,

[8] Lachmann (1978, 79ff) called this phenomenon a "division of capital" or an "increasing specialization of the processing function" and a "vertical disintegration of the capital structure".

[9] Interestingly, the original example from Adam Smith ([1776] 1993) about a pin factory is more in line with a vertical rather than a horizontal division of labour. This topic is also mentioned in Wicksell ([1893] 1954, p. 116).

[10] Only the method that produces the greatest output up to the specified length will be chosen.

[11] For example, making a stick and knocking down apples can take less time than climbing the tree directly (Murphy, 2003).

because it is not the most efficient among the methods of a given period of production. Some goods may even be impossible to produce using shorter methods (Böhm-Bawerk, 1891, p. 20). Therefore, in the rest of this analysis, we assume that only the most efficient methods for a specified length of the production process will be used.[12]

Even if we select a set of methods that produce the greatest output over a given period of time, further confusion can easily distort sound reasoning. Although the production of consumption goods takes more time with a longer process than with a shorter process, the fact that a longer process produces more consumption goods implies that a specified quantity of consumption goods is produced faster using a longer process; otherwise, it would be more efficient to produce the given output sequentially using the shorter process (Hayek, 1941, p. 77).

This idea is illustrated in Fig. 2.1. Panel (a) of the diagram depicts a very short process in which one unit of labour is employed for one period and produces one unit of a final consumption good. This process is repeated every period, so that five units of output are produced in five time periods and ten units of output in ten periods.

Panel (b) of Fig. 2.1 depicts a long roundabout process that produces a consumption good in five periods. One unit of labour is employed in each period, as in the first process. However, after five periods, this roundabout process produces ten units of output. Even though the same amount of labour is required, the output is greater because the process is longer—the input has been invested for a longer time until the final output has matured. The result of a longer process is thus a greater output per unit of input.

To illustrate the discussion using a similar depiction, we can imagine a third process that is as long as the second one (i.e. five periods), but which ultimately produces only four units of output. This process will never be chosen because it is inferior to the method in panel (b). It is also dominated by the first process, because it produces only four units of output after five periods, while the process in panel (a) yields one unit more when repeated five times.

[12] It would be more consistent with Hayek's approach to discuss the time a given input is invested in the production process (Hayek, 1941, pp. 69-70). Hence, only those methods will be chosen for which the given input will mature into the greatest possible output for the specified investment period of this input.

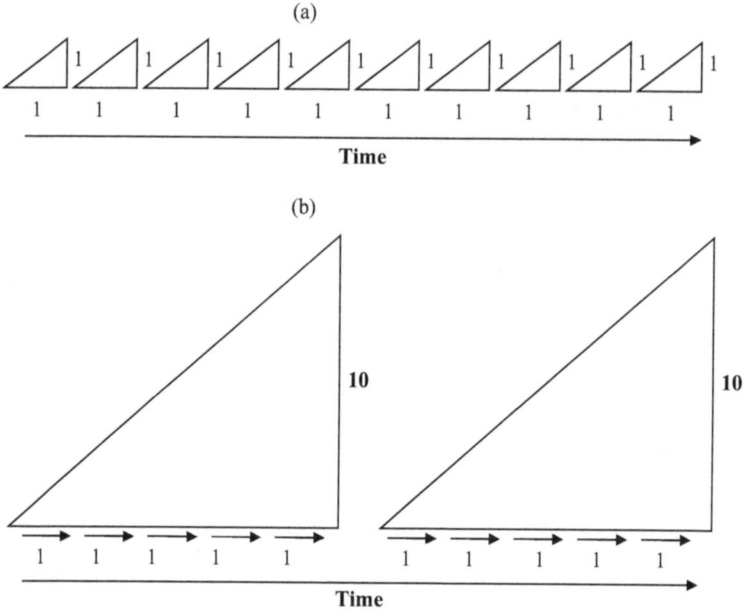

Fig. 2.1 Productivity of short and long processes. (**a**) A direct process. (**b**) A roundabout process

Much caution should be applied when identifying a long or short method. The first process in Fig. 2.1 is short in the sense that it produces final consumption goods in a shorter period of time. The second process is longer for the opposite reasons; one has to wait five periods before the consumption goods mature. However, it is more productive, because it produces not only more goods than the first process (this also applies to the inferior third process), but produces more goods in a comparable period of time. In addition, a specified amount of final consumption goods (ten units in this case) is produced faster, using the roundabout method in panel (b) (after five periods) than using the direct method in panel (a) (after ten periods).

Of these three methods, only the first and second are efficient. For the specified time periods in which final consumption goods are produced (one period and five periods), no other methods can be found that would produce greater output. The third process will not be chosen, because it is inefficient.

If a greater output is to be achieved, it is necessary to lengthen the production process. In other words, factors of production must be tied up in the process for a longer period of time. However, for this theory to have any definite meaning, it is necessary to assume that the knowledge in the economy for the relevant period is constant (Hayek, 1941, p. 72). This does not imply that all known inventions are utilized in current production processes. It only means that people know how a specific output can be produced using shorter and longer processes. They also understand that a longer process, which may employ other methods, create a different set of capital goods, and possibly apply better inventions, will ultimately produce greater output of consumer goods. However, it can happen that consumers still prefer shorter processes, even if they produce smaller quantities of consumption goods. In such a case, unused latent inventions, methods, and knowledge may exist that would lead to greater output using longer methods, but which are not utilized because consumers are not patient enough.[13]

Latent inventions, which can only be used in longer processes, may be a third reason for the higher productivity of roundabout methods. These inventions can be termed endogenous as they are instantly available in the economy. They should be distinguished from the inventions that are newly devised and that discover new methods of producing a specific or even greater quantity of consumption goods in a shorter time. This latter type can be called exogenous knowledge because it comes from outside and raises the existing level of technology in the economy. In Fig. 2.1, this can be illustrated by adding a new process that produces ten units of output in only four periods instead of five. Alternatively, the new invention discovers a method that produces 14 units in five periods, that is, 4 units more than the process in panel (b). This exogenous technical improvement is discussed in more detail in Chap. 7.[14]

[13] This idea is partly elaborated by Hayek (1941, p. 73), Mises (1996, p. 529), and Rothbard (2004). It should be stressed that the unused knowledge is not a symptom of inefficiency in the economy. Using latent technologies can be too costly in terms of "waiting for final product" to reach their full potential.

[14] The analysis is even more complicated when we realize that the inventions themselves do not fall from the sky. As the new growth theory has shown, investment is also needed to create new knowledge as in other manufacturing industries. In terms of Austrian capital theory, a long roundabout process must be launched to develop a new technology.

The question, then, is why production processes are not constantly lengthened, when longer methods provide greater outputs of consumer goods. The answer lies in two fundamental elements that limit time extensions of the production process. The first is based on the famous argument of diminishing marginal productivity. However, in the context of Austrian capital theory, this key economic principle may be difficult to grasp.[15] Although it was an integral part of Böhm-Bawerk's (1891, p. 84) work, Hayek (1941, 179 ff.) admitted that finding a suitable definition was relatively difficult and offered the following approach to the marginal product of capital: "[R]ate of increase of the product due to the extension of the investment period" (Hayek, 1941, p. 179).

It is generally believed that the marginal product (i.e. the marginal increase in consumer goods output) from the further extensions of the investment period should begin to decrease from some certain point. The basis for this assumption can be found in the three reasons mentioned earlier for higher productivity of roundabout processes.

First, further time extensions of the production process can gradually deplete hitherto unused natural resources and natural forces. It is conceivable that their physical contribution to the increase in output may be steadily declining. Second, the vertical division of labour and the resulting specialization, as well as the storehouse of knowledge and inventions used in longer processes as a third reason, can gradually lose their productive potential. Thus, all three reasons may begin to show diminishing marginal productivity from some certain point.[16]

This long exposition of the third reason for the existence of agio between present goods and future goods provides a basis for constructing an investment curve in the loanable funds market. It was separated from the first two causes, which are used to plot the upward-sloping saving curve. The assumptions that roundabout methods are more technically productive and that the output from the time extension of production grows at a decreasing rate (showing diminishing marginal productivity) lead to the conclusion that the investment curve is decreasing.

[15] Wicksell ([1901] 1977) demonstrated that the usual considerations of the marginal product of capital may lead to peculiar results.

[16] In Fig. 2.1, imagine a very long process that matures in ten periods and provides 24 units of output. The extension will again lead to greater output, but the marginal increase will fall. After ten periods, the output of the three methods will be 10, 20, and 24 units.

However, the diminishing marginal product is not sufficient to limit the indefinite extension of the production process. It is conceivable that even the slightest increase in future output may persuade entrepreneurs to extend the production process in time. The fundamental brake is provided by the first two Böhm-Bawerkian causes for the agio.

The fact that people underestimate their future needs or, as Mises (1996, p. 484) stated, that people prefer to enjoy satisfaction sooner rather than later limits the time extension of production. It restricts the numbers of factors of production that people are willing to allocate to longer processes. There must be a definite point at which an increase in future output will not be accepted at the expense of present output of consumer goods, because present satisfaction will be sought more urgently than a potential increase in future satisfaction. At this point, the time extension of the production process stops.

The effect of the first Böhm-Bawerkian reason for the existence of interest against unlimited lengthening is as follows. Because the time extension of the process requires that the factors of production be diverted from producing goods in the short term in favour of producing them in the more distant future, the output of present goods decreases, and the output of future goods increases. As a result, the relative provision of goods in the future improves at the expense of the present, which raises the marginal utility of present goods and reduces the marginal utility of future goods. People can become increasingly reluctant to give up present goods, even though the output of future goods grows as the production process lengthens. The sacrifice in present satisfaction will not be offset by the satisfaction gained by a greater amount of future goods. Therefore, the first cause can also end the lengthening of production methods. It is obvious that the two Böhm-Bawerkian causes operate in conformity.

The interaction of the three Böhm-Bawerkian reasons (greater provision in the future, underestimation of future wants, and superiority of longer methods) leads to a positive premium of present goods over future goods. This results in a positive interest rate in the economy, which limits the indefinite lengthening of the production process, because diminishing marginal product of capital, that is, decreasing increments of future output, cannot keep pace with the existing interest rate.[17]

[17] We return to this problem when we develop a model of loanable funds.

References

Endres, A. M. (1991). Austrian Capital and Interest Theory: Wieser's Contribution and the Menger Tradition. *The Review of Austrian Economics, 5*(1), 67–90.

Endres, A. M. (1997). *Neoclassical Microeconomic Theory: The Founding Austrian Version*. Routledge.

Fetter, F. A. (1928 [1915]). *Economics*. The Century Co.

Fisher, I. (1930). *Theory of Interest*. The Macmillan Company.

Jevons, W. S. (1957 [1871]). *The Theory of Political Economy*. Sentry Press.

Knight, F. H. (1936). The Quantity of Capital and the Rate of Interest: II. *The Journal of Political Economy, 44*(5), 612–642.

Lachmann, L. M. (1978 [1956]). *Capital and Its Structure*. Institute for Humane Studies.

Lewin, P. (1999). *Capital in Disequilibrium: The Role of Capital in a Changing World*. Routledge.

Lewin, P., & Cachanosky, N. (2019). *Austrian Capital Theory: A Modern Survey of the Essentials*. Cambridge University Press.

Lewin, P., & Cachanosky, N. (2021). *Capital and Finance: Theory and History*. Routledge.

Menger, C. (2007 [1871]). *Principles of Economics*. Ludwig von Mises Institute.

Murphy, R. P. (2003). *Unanticipated Intertemporal Change in Theories of Interest*. PhD Dissertation. New York University.

Potuzak, P. (2016a). Fisher and Mises on Zero Interest: A Reconsideration. *Prague Economic Papers, 25*(2), 202–220.

Potuzak, P. (2016b). *The Pure Time Preference Theory: A Neoclassical Critique*. Elsevier. Retrieved from SSRN: https://ssrn.com/abstract=2868789

Potuzak, P. (2016c). *What Can We Learn from the Böhm-Bawerkian Theory in the World of Zero Interest?* Elsevier. Retrieved from SSRN: https://ssrn.com/abstract=2865082

Rothbard, M. N. (2004 [1962]). *Man, Economy, and State*. Ludwig von Mises Institute.

Smith, A. (1993 [1776]). *An Inquiry into the Nature and Causes of the Wealth of Nations*. Oxford University Press.

von Böhm-Bawerk, E. (1890 [1884]). *Capital and Interest*. Macmillan and Co..

von Böhm-Bawerk, E. (1891 [1888]). *Positive Theory of Capital*. G. E. Stechert & Co.

von Hayek, F. A. (1941). *The Pure Theory of Capital*. The University of Chicago Press.

von Mises, L. (1996 [1949]). *Human Action: A Treatise on Economics* (4th ed.). Fox & Wilkes.

von Strigl, R. (2000 [1934]). *Capital and Production*. Ludwig von Mises Institute.

Wicksell, K. (1954 [1893]). *Value, Capital and Rent*. George Allen & Unwin Ltd.

Wicksell, K. (1977 [1901]). *Lectures on Political Economy, Volume 1*. Augustus M. Kelley Publishers.

CHAPTER 3

The Hayek Triangle

A useful tool that is widely used to describe the main principles of Austrian capital theory was developed by Hayek ([1931] 1935a), and further refined by Rothbard (2004), Garrison (2001), and Huerta de Soto ([1998] 2006). It was titled the Hayek triangle. This tool is a rough simplification of real processes in the economy. Even so, it can provide some important insights.[1]

Figure 3.1 illustrates one representative production process. The fact that production takes place over time is shown by a horizontal line. The vertical leg of the triangle measures the nominal value of the final consumption goods and portrays the ultimate objective of the entire production process. By cutting the triangle at any point in time and drawing a vertical line, the value of unfinished goods that are created on the way to the final consumption goods can be obtained.

The proceeds from the sale of a given intermediate product can be divided into three main components. First, the product of the previous stage, which is less processed, must be purchased. Second, the original means of production (i.e. labour and land) must be rewarded for their contribution to processing the product to the next stage. Finally, as

[1] Hayek ([1931] 1935a, p. 38) himself accepted Marschak's proposal to call this the Jevonian investment figure, because the triangle first appeared in the study by Jevons (1957). The evolution of macroeconomic models in the Austrian literature is described by Fillieule (2020).

P. Potuzak, *Austrian Theory of Capital and Business Cycle*,
https://doi.org/10.1007/978-3-031-18728-5_3

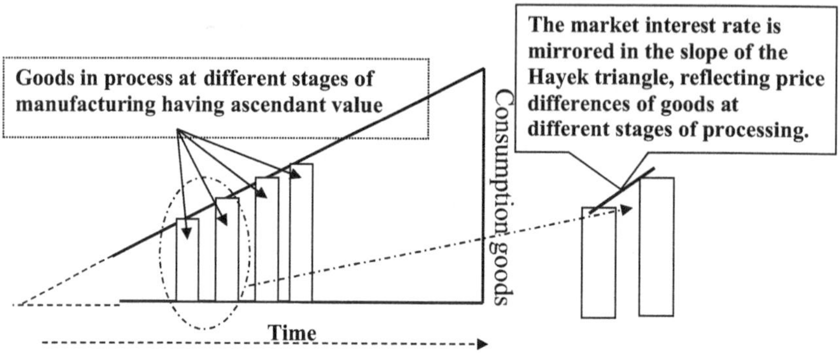

Fig. 3.1 The Hayek triangle

production progresses over time, future goods gradually mature to a stage closer to present goods, and therefore interest must accrue during the given period.

If the factors of production are added proportionally, the hypotenuse can be roughly represented by an exponential curve. However, this model is so stylized that even a linear line shows the most important features of the Austrian approach. In our analysis, the linear hypotenuse will therefore be used as a reasonable approximation. A more important property than the exact shape of the hypotenuse is that the further the phase is from the final consumption goods, the lower the value of the intermediate product will be.

The beginning of the triangle is not very important either, because it is impossible to discern when the specific process of creating consumption goods began.[2] Therefore, it would be sensible to depict the triangle with an open beginning. This approach is also supported by the fact that the history of the production process is never important: all processes are in essence forward-looking (Kirzner, 1966, p. 79). Entrepreneurs never look back in time when buying intermediate products and other capital goods. They never ask about the past of a particular capital good (Mises, 1996). It is primarily a matter of optimally combining factors of production and choosing the optimum length of the production process to maximize profits.

[2] This objection was raised especially by Knight (1934, 1935a, 1935b, 1936a, 1936b).

In contrast, the slope of the Hayek triangle is particularly important. It displays the value difference between the adjacent stages of production. As noted, future goods have a lower value than present goods. The further a given stage is from final consumption, the more distant are the future goods it represents, and the lower is its value. As the process gradually approaches production of final consumption goods, the value of intermediate products increases. The no-arbitrage condition then requires a uniform percentage difference in value between adjacent stages, assuming identical production time in each phase.

The horizontal line of the Hayek triangle represents the duration of the roundabout process. Due to the diminishing marginal productivity of roundabout methods, and because of the first two Böhm-Bawerkian causes that restrict their lengthening, it is perfectly clear that the lower the agio between present and future goods, the longer the process can be. In other words, if people are more patient and their time preference is thus lower, they are ready to wait for the consumable output for a longer time, and the production process may be more roundabout.

The process depicted in Fig. 3.2 has a smaller slope of the hypotenuse because lower impatience narrows the agio between present and future goods. It is consistent with the lower interest rate in the economy, which enables a longer production method. In contrast, if the valuation of present goods far exceeds the valuation of future goods, that is, if people show a considerable time preference, the slope of the triangle will be large. The resulting high interest rate will restrict the potential roundaboutness of the production process, as shown in Fig. 3.3.

However, Figs. 3.2 and 3.3 can be misleading. At first glance, the process in Fig. 3.3 appears to produce greater quantities of final consumption goods than the process in Fig. 3.2. As discussed, the exact opposite is true, because a longer method should result in greater output. The triangles in

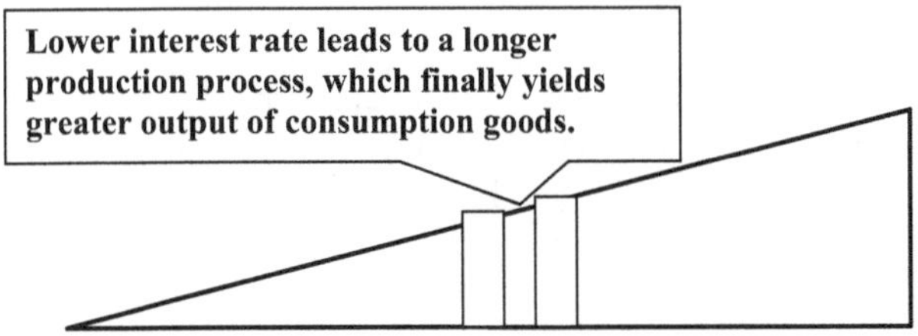

Fig. 3.2 Production process for a low interest rate

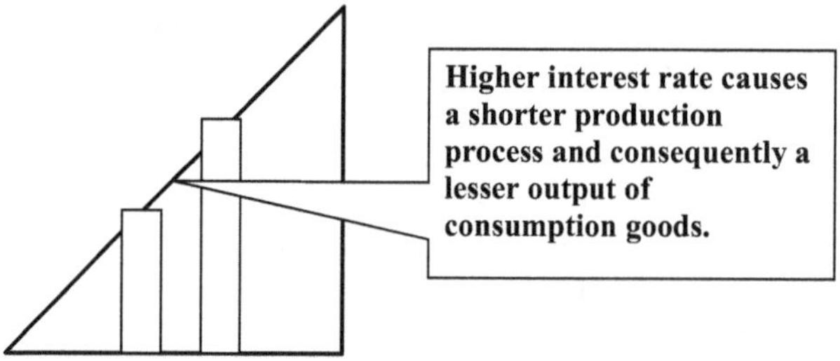

Fig. 3.3 Production process for a high interest rate

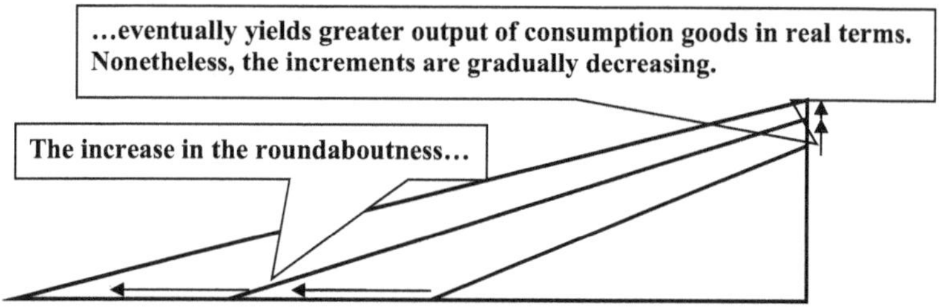

Fig. 3.4 Decreasing marginal productivity of the roundabout process

Figs. 3.2 and 3.3 are constructed in nominal terms, so the size of the vertical leg does not reflect the actual total output of the real consumption goods.

A picture that is more consistent with Austrian theory is depicted in Fig. 3.4. Here, the final output, represented by the vertical leg, is measured in real terms rather than in nominal terms. Figure 3.4 shows that a more roundabout process produces greater output. The triangle also plots the decreasing marginal productivity of the additional lengthening of the production process.

It can be instructive to look again at the Hayek triangle. Analysis indicates that the production process can be quite fragile. Each stage must be perfectly connected to the previous stage. If one phase is disrupted or stopped, the entire process will collapse, and consumption goods will not be completed.

However, the price system and profit-seeking behaviour should mitigate a catastrophic scenario if one stage of the process is eliminated. Figure 3.5 shows what happens if one stage of the production process is

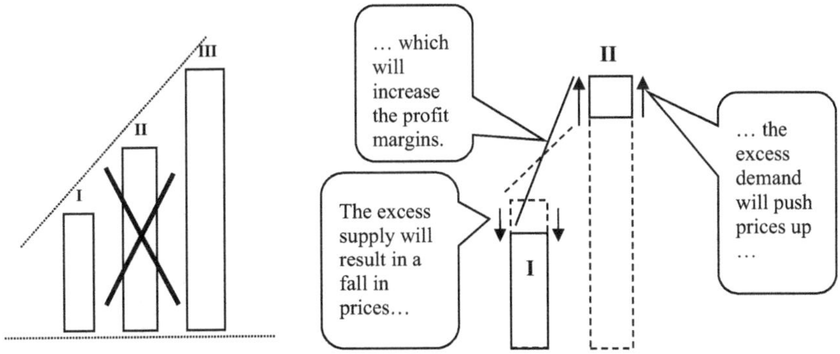

Fig. 3.5 Elimination of one stage in the production process

removed. Sooner or later, the preceding stage will experience a drastic fall in demand, which will lead to a drop in the price of its output. The stage that follows the eliminated stage will be hit with an immense shortage of inputs, which will drive up the price of the reduced output of the stage that has been removed. The price difference between the stages will sky-rocket and create above-normal profits for every entrepreneur who enters at the removed stage. As a result, the suspension of production in one stage should quickly attract profit-seeking entrepreneurs, and a smooth production process will eventually be restored. Once it is resumed, the value difference between two successive stages will be uniform for the entire production process. A single interest rate will again prevail in the economy.

The Hayek triangle introduced here represents a special type of process known as the continuous input-point output model. Final consumption goods are created via gradual addition of factors of production. All capital goods have only the form of intermediate products, that is, goods in process. According to Hayek (1941), such a model is particularly suitable for describing the nature of capital theory.

We assumed that the only material input in each stage came from the preceding stage, and no resources other than land and labour were used. This approach is far removed from reality. Suppose that some stage also buys products from other processes. Obviously, many of these products also went through a time-consuming method of production. Figure 3.6 shows a more complex picture of the economy. The time required to produce the intermediate product that is used in the major process must also

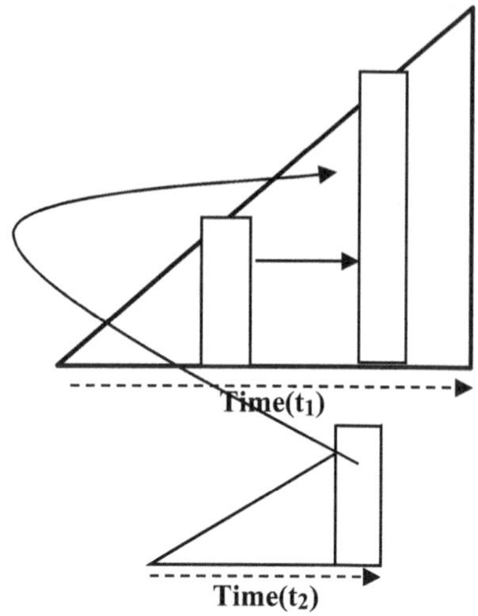

Fig. 3.6 Input being produced in another roundabout process

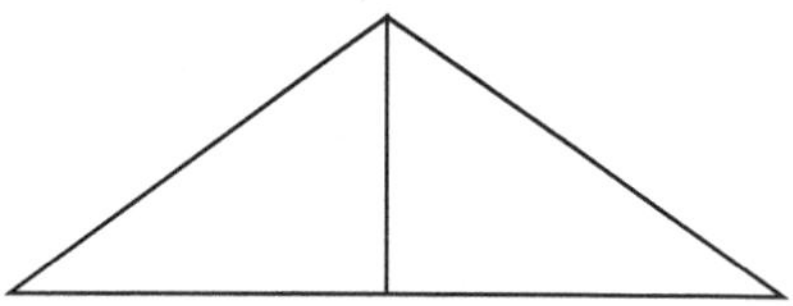

Fig. 3.7 Continuous input-continuous output scheme

be calculated, which makes it even more difficult to accurately express the length of the main process.

Material inputs from other processes can be inserted into any stage, so the overall picture of the production structure will be infinitely complex and almost incomprehensible. The price system must also guarantee synchronization in the sense that the required input for the main process should be prepared at the right time. It is obvious that the longer the period that is needed to produce a given input (t_2 in Fig. 3.6), the higher will be the ability and accuracy needed on the part of entrepreneurs to keep the production process running smoothly. Price signals play a fundamental role in this synchronization.

The foregoing analysis set aside durable capital goods and durable consumption goods. The economic essence of consumer durables was first illustrated by Jevons (1957, p. 231), who added another triangle to the first. Such a process is a type of continuous input-continuous output scheme. This approach is shown in Fig. 3.7, in which the descending shape

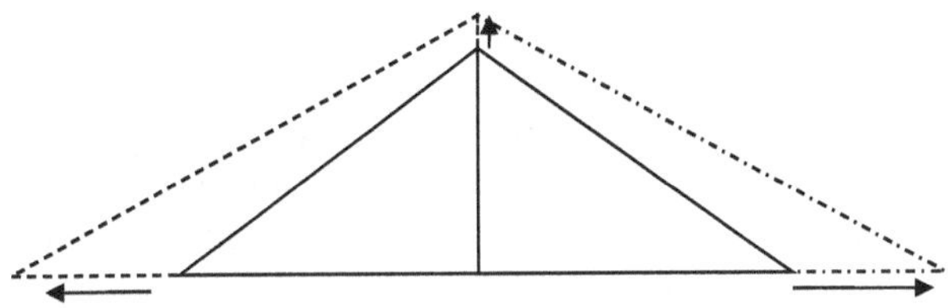

Fig. 3.8 Continuous input-continuous output scheme in real terms for lower time preferences

of the second triangle reflects the flow of services of a durable consumption good that gradually fades out over time.

Suppose that the agio between present goods and future goods, that is, the interest rate, decreases. This will also flatten the second triangle. There are two fundamental reasons for its changing shape. First, the flow of services of durable consumer goods will be discounted at a lower rate. Second, lower impatience in the production process usually leads to the creation of consumption goods with higher durability. This fact was documented, for example, by Fisher (1930). Figure 3.8 represents two continuous input-continuous output processes in real terms, where the flatter one is consistent with a lower interest rate.

Another complication in this analysis is the inclusion of a durable capital good, which can be used at any stage of the production process. The durable capital good is not fully utilized in one period, because it can provide services continuously over time. It is also the product of a time-consuming process, in which the durability of a capital good usually depends on the time spent creating it.

Given the fundamental characteristics of the production process in the real world, even a simple Hayek triangle of continuous input-point output can provide important insights. In particular, the figure clarifies that capital cannot be considered a homogenous amorphous aggregate.[3] It does not make much sense to add up the value of all the products at different stages of processing. Any attempt to calculate the fixed relationship between the value of capital and its size is futile. In contrast to labour and land, the amount of capital changes if the market data change, that is, the prices of materials or the rate of interest. For a given set of prices and the

[3] In this context, the discussion between Hayek and Knight on the nature of capital is especially instructive. See, for example, Hayek (1935b, 1936a) and Knight (1935a).

interest rate, one production process may represent a higher amount of capital, while for another price structure, the aggregate value of another process may indicate a higher quantity of capital (Hayek, 1935b, p. 242).[4]

The Austrian authors therefore consider capital to be a heterogeneous phenomenon, the total value of which is of little importance. Economic science should explore its components and the relationships between them, rather than the aggregate quantity of capital (Hayek, 1941, p. 6; Lachmann, 1978, p. 2). Only a thorough analysis of the links between various capital goods, their potential complementarity and consistency for production processes can provide the necessary insights into the functioning of complex modern economies. As shown later, such an approach is crucial in the analysis of business cycle. Thinking of capital as an aggregated and amorphous mass tends to blur the real existing processes. In this context, Hayek offered the following definition of the supply of capital:

> *The datum usually called the "supply of capital" can thus be adequately described only in terms of the totality of all the alternative income streams between which the existence of a certain stock of nonpermanent resources (together with the expected flow of input) enables us to choose.*
> Hayek (1941, p. 147)

Hayek also emphasized another feature of capital that other economists, most notably Frank Knight, deliberately disregarded or even rejected. For Hayek, capital is a set of non-permanent resources that must be maintained, restored, or replaced to ensure the flow of income (or the output of consumption goods) at a given constant level (Hayek, 1941, p. 88, 1936a, p. 201). Although capital goods can provide a permanent flow of income, they are not permanent resources per se. Only when capital goods are properly maintained is their production power secured.

In contrast, according to Knight (1934, p. 264), the replacement of capital goods is just a technical detail that is not worthy of any economic analysis. However, even the simple continuous input-point output process

[4] For instance, 12 workers are always more than 10 workers regardless of the wage rate. However, as capital can only be measured in terms of value, a change in prices can reverse which production process represents a greater quantity of capital. Thus, the Austrians demonstrated the problems associated with capital theory much earlier than the famous Cambridge capital controversy (Samuelson, 1966). The connection between this controversy and Austrian capital theory is discussed by Rosser (2020), Fratini (2019), and Lewin and Cachanosky (2019).

in Fig. 3.5 shows that such an approach is highly problematic. If any stage of the production process is not maintained, the smooth flow of consumption goods can be endangered. Furthermore, it is not an easy task for entrepreneurs to decide where and in what quantities the factors of production should be allocated. It cannot be taken for granted that investments will always be made in the necessary amounts. Thus, maintaining capital is not a simple technical detail that is unrelated to human action. Without a planning entrepreneur and a functioning price system, the replacement of capital goods is never guaranteed.

In a discussion with Knight, Hayek (1935b) showed that, without reference to the flow of income provided by a given set of capital goods and preferred by the consumer, the concept of maintaining capital intact is problematic. According to Hayek, when data change, sometimes a reduction in capital, and sometimes an increase (in value terms), is essential to keep the flow of income from capital at the previous level. In other words, simply maintaining a stable level of capital in terms of its value may not be sufficient to ensure its productive power. In addition, because capital goods are usually replaced by other units, it is difficult to distinguish which part of the investment is merely a replacement for the depreciated capital and what is related to its net increase.

According to Knight (1934), the focus of economics should be on studying a net increase in the total capital stock in the economy. Replacement of depreciated capital goods is a simple technical detail. By contrast, for Hayek, the decision of an acting entrepreneur about the net investment in his capital stock is inseparable from his decision about a "mere" replacement. As a result, the theoretical separation of the replacement of capital goods and net investment is of little importance. It is rather a symptom of unsound economic reasoning. Both types of investment require a calculating entrepreneur who makes decisions based on relevant prices and interest rates. The "mere" replacement of capital goods is thus never a simple technical detail, because it is not automatically secured from the flow of returns to capital.

The third controversy between Hayek and Knight is important for further analysis and can be illustrated on the Hayek triangle. So far, we have analysed one production process of a given length and its productivity. In a stationary economy, or what Mises (1996) called an evenly rotating economy, specified processes and operations required to produce intermediate products are repeated in the same way using the same methods. The cross-section picture of the economy is thus essentially the same as the

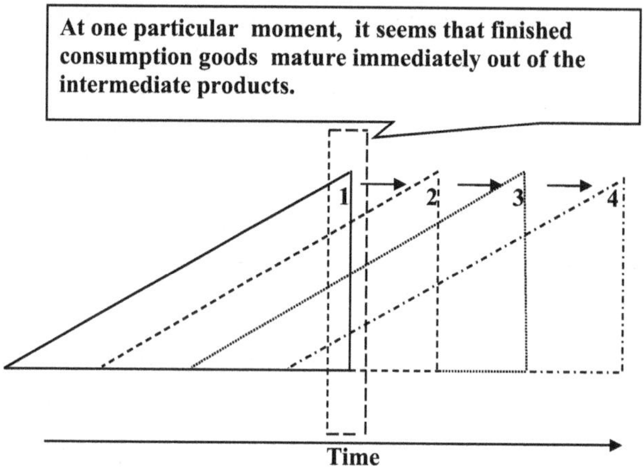

Fig. 3.9 Spurious synchronization of the production processes

image over time. At every moment, a very similar set of capital goods is produced, whether in the present, in the past, or in the future. In each period, a whole range of different intermediate products in various stages of processing is produced. Many processes at different stages of completion can be observed. Some are maturing as final consumption goods, others are almost ready, some are midway in the process, and others have only recently begun.

This picture of a stationary capital-using economy can be delineated in Fig. 3.9, which is a simplified version of the three-dimensional model developed by Hayek (1941, p. 117).[5] At first glance, one can be misled by a mistake that could be called the "Clark-Knight fallacy". At one particular moment, the cross-section of this system of triangles seems to make the production process negligibly short, as if it lasted only one period. Production and consumption seem to be synchronous. However, this interpretation would be misleading. Intermediate products will never transform into consumption goods instantly, without requiring some production time. The exact opposite is true. The processes that have just been

[5] It would be possible to reproduce the whole three-dimensional model. Although our figure lacks one dimension, and therefore lacks one feature of the production process, it seems to capture the most important characteristics of the production process from the point of view of Austrian capital theory.

initiated will only mature after a considerable time (triangle 4 in Fig. 3.9). Those at a higher stage of completion will result in final consumption goods sooner (e.g. triangle 2 or 3), and processes that began in the distant past may very shortly offer completed consumption goods (triangle 1).

It is therefore clear that a process that has just matured into final consumption goods was not initiated in the recent past. Although its entire history cannot be traced, most operations performed on present consumer goods were carried out in the past. The relative importance of the previous stages depends on the degree of roundaboutness, which corresponds to the time preferences of consumers. It also determines the productivity and quantity of final consumption goods produced by this method.[6]

If we focus on the processes running in the present, it is obvious that only a small part of the original means of production (i.e. labour and land) is devoted to the completion of final consumption goods. The labour force is allocated to processes that mature at different dates in the future. This finding should also be consistent with the relative value of the various forms of intermediate products manufactured by labour. In other words, at a given time, the total value of intermediate goods should be much higher than the value of final consumption goods. The major part of the potential wealth of a society is in the form of products that will mature in the future, rather than in the form of finished consumption goods.

Another important fact is that, although only a minority of workers are allocated in the final consumption stage, their output is significantly higher than if the total labour force were devoted to creating consumable output by direct methods. The reason obviously lies in the greater productivity of the roundabout methods, which have a fundamental advantage in that the labour and land implemented in the past are "stored" in the intermediate products that will be completed in a given period (Böhm-Bawerk, 1891; Wicksell, 1977a). Another logical consequence of the analysis is that the richer the society is, and the more roundabout methods it uses, the higher the share of work in progress on the existing quantity of goods.[7]

[6] In the analysis of the business cycle in Chap. 5, we are particularly interested in triangles (or different types of triangles) that will mature in the future (or at different times in the future, depending on the time preferences of consumers, which will determine the degree of roundaboutness and thus productivity). Our approach is again forward-looking.

[7] Even if roundabout processes are not initiated, ongoing production can ensure an uninterrupted flow of consumption goods for some time. A shortage of consumption goods will thus arise after a certain period of time. The flow of goods will decrease only slowly, because the stocks of products in progress will diminish only gradually (Rothbard, 2004).

Total expenditures on unfinished goods of various forms are significantly higher in a given period of time (e.g. 1 year) than total expenditures on final goods, even though the price of consumer goods (vertical leg) is the highest in the Hayek triangle. The reason is that future consumption goods, which currently take the form of raw materials, semi-finished products, goods in wholesale warehouses, and so forth, change hands many times before they mature into a form that is ready for direct consumption (Hayek, 1935a).

Several observations made so far, especially with regard to the interest rate, can be illustrated by the neoclassical model of loanable funds introduced into the Austrian analysis by Garrison (2001).[8] Although capital theory should be explored in a dynamic environment, this model can be helpful for disciplining one's thinking, as it can easily be trapped in vicious circles.

Garrison (2001, p. 50) plotted a simple Marshallian diagram in which a downward-sloping investment curve intersects at one point with an upward-sloping saving curve. This intersection depicts the equilibrium interest rate in the market of loanable funds. It also shows the equilibrium quantity of loanable funds, where saving equals investment. Before explaining equilibrium and its connection to the Hayek triangle, it is necessary to discuss the forces that may be behind both curves, because plotting a simple supply and demand diagram does not solve the problem of determining the interest rate, but rather introduces it. As Fisher put it:

> *To say that the rate of interest is fixed by supply and demand is merely to state, not to solve the problem. Every competitive price is fixed by supply and demand. The real problem is to analyze the particular supply and demand forces.*
> Fisher (1930, p. 46)

An upward-sloping saving curve may represent a gradually increasing rate of time preference (or impatience), as more present goods are offered for longer processes. Only an increase in the rate of interest can persuade savers to further postpone their consumption to the future. In other words, savers require greater and greater quantities of future goods as they sacrifice additional units of present goods. This explanation is consistent

[8] A critique of Garrison's approach can be found in Hülsmann (2001) and Fillieule (2005), and a critique of Hayek triangles appears in Barnett and Block (2006).

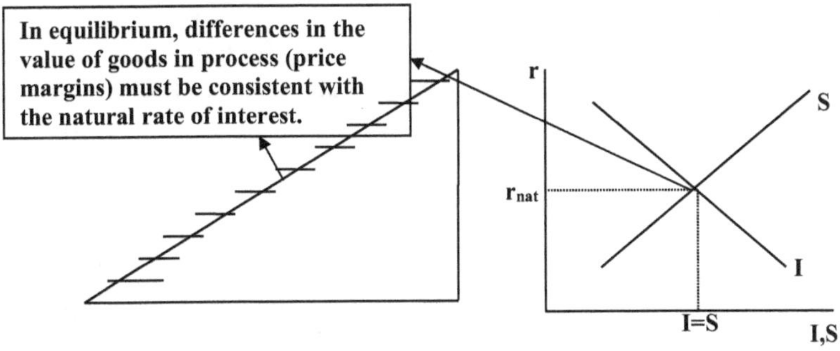

Fig. 3.10 The loanable funds market and the Hayek triangle

with the first two causes of interest outlined by Böhm-Bawerk. A more detailed analysis appears in Potuzak (2016a, 2016b, 2016c).

The decreasing investment curve may reflect the third reason for the existence of interest and the diminishing marginal productivity of roundabout processes. Every extension of roundabout methods will result in greater consumer goods output; however, marginal increases will gradually decline. Therefore, if the interest rate is too high, it is not profitable to continue further lengthening, because investment becomes less attractive.

The investment curve is above zero in Fig. 3.10, which can be explained as a non-negative marginal product approaches zero only with an infinite extension of the production process.[9] Boundless lengthening is blocked by the time preference of consumers, which condenses the first two causes of interest. In other words, the time extension of production processes is limited by the positive interest rate prevailing in the economy.[10]

This Fisherian approach would not be accepted by many important authors writing in the Austrian tradition. Mises (1996), Rothbard (2004), and Garrison (1979), who himself introduced this model into Austrian theory, all adhere to the approach of Fetter (1902, 1928), who emphasized time preference as the only interest rate factor, and denied any role of roundaboutness (i.e. productivity) in determining the interest rate. For these authors, productivity is secondary because productivity changes can only affect the interest rate temporarily. In the near future, interest rates should return to a level determined solely by time preference. Moreover,

[9] This property is in line with one of the Inada conditions (Romer, 2006).

[10] A negative interest rate is discussed in Potuzak (2016a, 2016b, 2016c).

according to these authors, the founder of Austrian capital theory, Böhm-Bawerk (1890, 1891), contradicted himself in the sense that, in his first book, he convincingly demolished (naïve) productivity theories, while in the second, he reintroduced the element of productivity under the guise of roundabout methods (Fetter, 1902).[11]

On the other hand, Hayek (1936b, 1941) favoured the productivity element and accepted the objections of Knight (1936a, 1936b), especially against the idea of underestimating future needs. Although Hayek (1945) eventually modified his view and gave time preference crucial importance at the end of an unsustainable boom, his emphasis on the productivity of investments in determining the interest rate is ubiquitous in his theory.

Potuzak (2016a, 2016b, 2016c) deals with this controversy in more detail. In this chapter, a compromise version is accepted, which is perhaps most consistent with the original Böhm-Bawerkian interpretation and consonant with Fisherian analysis.[12] Therefore, assume that both elements, time preference and productivity, determine the interest rate. A simple loanable funds model presented in this chapter is used to explain their role.

This approach suggests that the interest rate is a real, rather than a monetary, phenomenon, as it is determined by the flow of real saving and real investment. The intersection of the two curves is crucial. The equilibrium interest rate at which saving is in line with investment is usually called the natural rate of interest. Its most cited definition, by Knut Wicksell, states:

> *The rate of interest at which the demand for loan capital and the supply of savings exactly agree, and which more or less corresponds to the expected yield on the newly created capital, will then be the normal or natural real rate.*
> Wicksell ([1906] 1977b, p. 193)

Wicksell modified the definition he proposed in his earlier work:

> *There is a certain rate of interest on loans which is neutral in respect to commodity prices, and tends neither to raise nor to lower them. This is necessarily*

[11] The pure time preference approach of Austrian authors can be found in Herbener (2011). On the other hand, Murphy (2003) showed that Böhm-Bawerk is perfectly consistent and that his theory was misinterpreted by the authors mentioned above. A detailed critique of pure time preference theory appears in Potuzak (2016a, 2016b, 2016c).

[12] Fisher (1930) himself attributed this explanation to Böhm-Bawerk, although from his point of view, Böhm-Bawerk's inclusion of productivity was somewhat confusing and misleading.

the same as the rate of interest which would be determined by supply and demand if no use were made of money and all lending were effected in the form of real capital goods. It comes to much the same thing to describe it as the current value of the natural rate of interest on capital.
Wicksell ([1898] 1936, p. 102)

This interest rate should also reflect the agio between present goods and future goods. It must be consistent with the slope of the Hayek triangle as shown in Fig. 3.10. Suppose that the interest rate on the loanable funds market is lower than in the Hayek triangle. This means that the value difference between present consumption goods and present factors of production (i.e. future goods) is higher than the interest rate on the market for loanable funds.[13] There will be an incentive to borrow on the loanable funds market and take advantage of this profit opportunity. Increased demand on the market will raise the interest rate, which will eventually stabilize at the level prevailing in the processes of the structure of production.

For some Austrian authors, the loanable funds market is only secondary compared to the difference in values between present and future goods (Salerno, 2001). However, this model reflects agio and may shed more light on complicated processes than the Hayek triangle for analyses of some features of the business cycle. This chapter therefore uses both tools, bearing in mind their limitations and disadvantages.

The variable as important as the natural interest rate on the vertical axis appears on the horizontal axis. As Fig. 3.10 shows, for a specific natural interest rate, the flow of real investment equals the flow of real saving. This exact amount of investment is necessary to maintain the production process. The economy creates precisely the amount of new capital needed to preserve a continuous and undisturbed process of production, to maintain a specific shape and size of the Hayek triangle. The length of the production process is then optimal, because the existing time-extension of production is perfectly consistent with time preferences of consumers. At the margin, the first and second Böhm-Bawerkian causes for interest are in line with the third cause.

[13] This sentence should be slightly reformulated to make the theory more consistent. The interest rate must be compared with the difference between the value of present factors of production and the (future) value of consumption goods that will be produced by them. However, in the stationary economy that has been analysed thus far, the value of consumption goods is the same at all times.

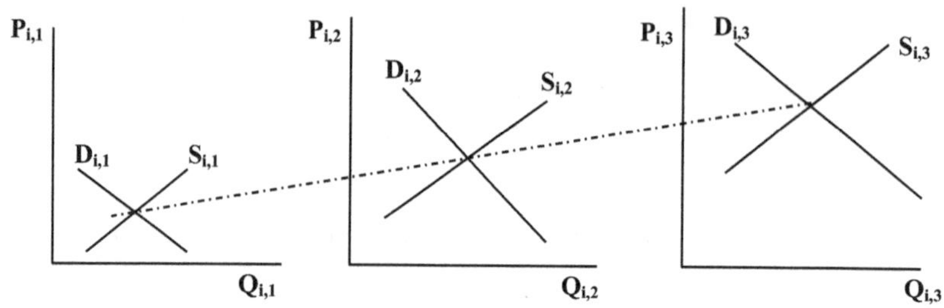

Fig. 3.11 Markets of production goods at different stages of completion

At the end of this chapter, a system of graphs within the Hayek triangle is created, which will be useful for analysing the processes when the economy is being restructured, whether for real or monetary reasons. Representative markets of work in progress in the Hayek triangle are depicted in Fig. 3.11. This illustrates Hayek's idea that capital goods are mainly production goods in process (Q_i), which eventually mature into consumption goods (Q_c). Each good in process ($Q_{i,1}$; $Q_{i,2}$; $Q_{i,3}$; …) has its own market, with its own market price. The price of the production good that is further from the final consumption stage is lower than the price of the good in process that is closer to it. Price margins between goods at different stages of completion reflect the slope of the Hayek triangle. They are also consistent with the natural interest rate.

The supply side of each market is composed of firms operating at different stages of production. Although demand in each market is driven by firms producing intermediate goods at the subsequent stage, key players on this side of the markets need to be sought elsewhere, specifically at the end of the production process. When identifying the main drivers of demand for production goods, it is necessary to be aware of the economic nature of these goods. As demonstrated, production goods are future consumption goods. Therefore, the demand for them is driven by individuals who demand future consumption goods. These people are savers, because saving represents the demand for consumer goods that will mature at some point in the future.

References

Barnett, W., II, & Block, W. (2006). On Hayekian Triangles. *Procesos De Mercado: Revista Europea De Economia Politica, III*(2), 39–141.

Fetter, F. A. (1902). The "Roundabout Process" in the Interest Theory. *The Quarterly Journal of Economics, 17*(1), 163–180.

Fetter, F. A. (1928 [1915]). *Economics*. The Century Co..

Fillieule, R. (2005). The "Value-Riches" Model: An Alternative to Garrison's Model in Austrian Macroeconomics of Growth and Cycle. *The Quarterly Journal of Austrian Economics, 8*(2), 3–19.

Fillieule, R. (2020). The Macroeconomic Models of the Austrian School: A History and Comparative Analysis. *The Quarterly Journal of Austrian Economics, 22*(4), 533–564.

Fisher, I. (1930). *Theory of Interest*. The Macmillan Company.

Fratini, S. M. (2019). A Note on Re-switching, the Average Period of Production and the Austrian Business-Cycle Theory. *The Review of Austrian Economics, 32*, 363–374.

Garrison, R. W. (1979). In Defense of the Misesian Theory of Interest. *Journal of Libertarian Studies, 3*(2), 141–150.

Garrison, R. W. (2001). *Time and Money, the Macroeconomics of Capital Structure*. Routledge.

Herbener, J. M. (Ed.). (2011). *The Pure Time-Preference Theory of Interest*. Ludwig von Mises Institute.

Huerta de Soto, J. (2006 [1998]). *Money, Bank Credit, and Economic Cycles*. Ludwig von Mises Institute.

Hülsmann, J. G. (2001). Garrisonian Macroeconomics. *The Quarterly Journal of Austrian Economics, 4*(3), 33–41.

Jevons, W. S. (1957 [1871]). *The Theory of Political Economy*. Sentry Press.

Kirzner, I. (1966). *An Essay on Capital*. Augustus M. Kelly.

Knight, F. H. (1934). Capital, Time, and the Interest Rate. *Economica, 1*(3), 257–286.

Knight, F. H. (1935a). Professor Hayek and the Theory of Investment. *The Economic Journal, 45*(177), 77–94.

Knight, F. H. (1935b). The Theory of Investment Once More: Mr. Boulding and the Austrians. *The Quarterly Journal of Economics, 50*(1), 36–67.

Knight, F. H. (1936a). The Quantity of Capital and the Rate of Interest: I. *The Journal of Political Economy, 44*(4), 433–463.

Knight, F. H. (1936b). The Quantity of Capital and the Rate of Interest: II. *The Journal of Political Economy, 44*(5), 612–642.

Lachmann, L. M. (1978 [1956]). *Capital and Its Structure*. Institute for Humane Studies.

Lewin, P., & Cachanosky, N. (2019). Re-switching, the Average Period of Production and the Austrian Business-Cycle Theory: A Comment on Fratini. *The Review of Austrian Economics, 32*, 375–382.

Murphy, R. P. (2003). *Unanticipated Intertemporal Change in Theories of Interest*. Ph.D. Dissertation, New York University

Potuzak, P. (2016a). Fisher and Mises on Zero Interest: A Reconsideration. *Prague Economic Papers, 25*(2), 202–220.

Potuzak, P. (2016b). *The Pure Time Preference Theory: A Neoclassical Critique*. Elsevier. Retrieved from SSRN: https://ssrn.com/abstract=2868789
Potuzak, P. (2016c). *What Can We Learn from the Böhm-Bawerkian Theory in the World of Zero Interest?* Elsevier. Retrieved from SSRN: https://ssrn.com/abstract=2865082
Romer, D. (2006). *Advanced Macroeconomics* (3rd ed.). McGraw–Hill.
Rosser, J. B. (2020). Austrian themes and the Cambridge capital theory controversies. *The Review of Austrian Economics, 33*, 415–431.
Rothbard, M. N. (2004 [1962]). *Man, Economy, and State*. Ludwig von Mises Institute.
Salerno, J. T. (2001). Does the Concept of Secular Growth Have a Place in Capital-Based Macroeconomics? *The Quarterly Journal of Austrian Economics, 4*(3), 43–61.
Samuelson, P. A. (1966). A Summing Up. *The Quarterly Journal of Economics, 80*(4), 568–583.
von Böhm-Bawerk, E. (1890 [1884]). *Capital and Interest*. The Macmillan Company.
von Böhm-Bawerk, E. (1891 [1888]). *Positive Theory of Capital*. G. E. Stechert & Co.
von Hayek, F. A. (1935a [1931]). *Prices and Production* (2nd ed.). Augustus M. Kelly.
von Hayek, F. A. (1935b). The Maintenance of Capital. *Economica, 2*(7), 241–276.
von Hayek, F. A. (1936a). The Mythology of Capital. *Quarterly Journal of Economics, 50*(2), 199–228.
von Hayek, F. A. (1936b). Utility Analysis and Interest. *The Economic Journal, 46*(181), 44–60.
von Hayek, F. A. (1941). *The Pure Theory of Capital*. The University of Chicago Press.
von Hayek, F. A. (1945). Time-Preference and Productivity: A Reconsideration. *Economica, 12*(45), 22–25.
von Mises, L. (1996 [1949]). *Human Action: A Treatise on Economics* (4th ed.). Fox & Wilkes.
Wicksell, K. (1936 [1898]). *Interest and Prices*. Augustus M. Kelley.
Wicksell, K. (1977a [1901]). *Lectures on Political Economy, Volume 1*. Augustus M. Kelley.
Wicksell, K. (1977b [1906]). *Lectures on Political Economy, Volume 2*. Augustus M. Kelley.

CHAPTER 4

A Decrease in Time Preference

The tools developed in the previous chapters are sufficient to describe the nature of the process that transforms the Hayek triangle from one shape (Fig. 3.3) to another (Fig. 3.2 in Chap. 3), and illuminate what is known as a change in the roundabout method of production.

According to standard economic models, individuals try to adjust the time shape of their consumption to maximize utility. As Fisher (1930) demonstrated, the optimum stream of the consumption of an individual depends on factors including the time shape of income, the average level of income, the composition of income, the interest rate, the time preference, the degree of risk in different periods, and many other factors. At this stage, we are not interested in either the main determinants that affect the specific flow of individual consumption, nor are we concerned with the response of the individual to these factors. The main goal of this section is to determine whether Austrian theory is well designed for the analysis of mechanisms in the structure of production and the roundabout processes, when a large number of individuals change their optimal allocation of consumption over time.

Consider a change in the optimal consumption path such that a large percentage of consumers reallocate their income stream in favour of consumption in more distant periods in the future at the expense of the present and the near future. In other words, suppose that, in an economy, the relative demand between present consumption goods and future

P. Potuzak, *Austrian Theory of Capital and Business Cycle*,
https://doi.org/10.1007/978-3-031-18728-5_4

Fig. 4.1 Decrease in time preference in the loanable funds market

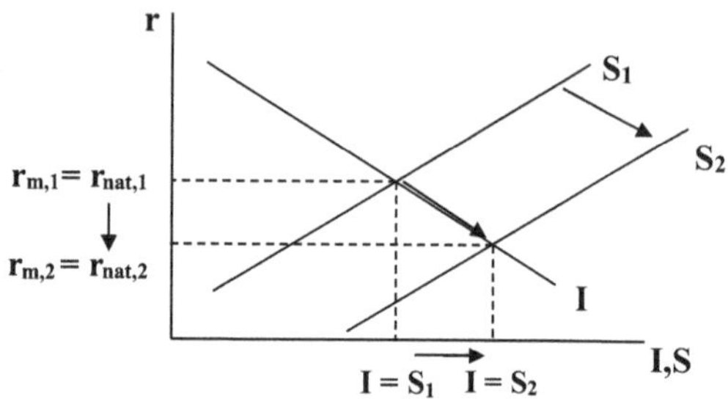

consumption goods shifts towards the future at the expense of the present. Simply put, people's time preference falls exogenously, and they start saving more.

Reduced demand for present consumption goods will first be observed in the stages producing goods for immediate usage and in the stages very close to final consumption, while earlier stages creating production goods should experience an increase in demand, as new saving representing demand for future goods is channelled to this part of the production process. However, the new saving would have never found its way into the earlier stages of production if the interest rate had not fallen. In other words, the initial phase of this mechanism hinges on the assumption that an increase in saving will lead to a reduction in the interest rate.

Figure 4.1 shows that both the natural (r_{nat}) and the market (r_m) interest rates decrease. This decline in the interest rate will encourage investment expenditures. If something blocks the smooth transformation of saving into investment, the next steps of the mechanism cannot continue, and the structure of production can never be fully transformed. This discrepancy could be illustrated in Fig. 4.1 by a fall in the natural rate of interest and a constant market rate that would not follow the path of the natural rate ($r_{m,1} > r_{\text{nat},2}$), which would lead to an excess of saving over investment.[1]

If the process operates without disturbances, the inflow of saving to earlier stages will be reflected in an increase in demand for production goods. The resulting higher prices will encourage supply to meet this expanded demand, as shown in the left panel of Fig. 4.2. The crucial

[1] This assumption is relaxed in Potuzak (2021), who analyses the behaviour of the economy when part of the saved income is not invested but hoarded, that is, retained in money balances.

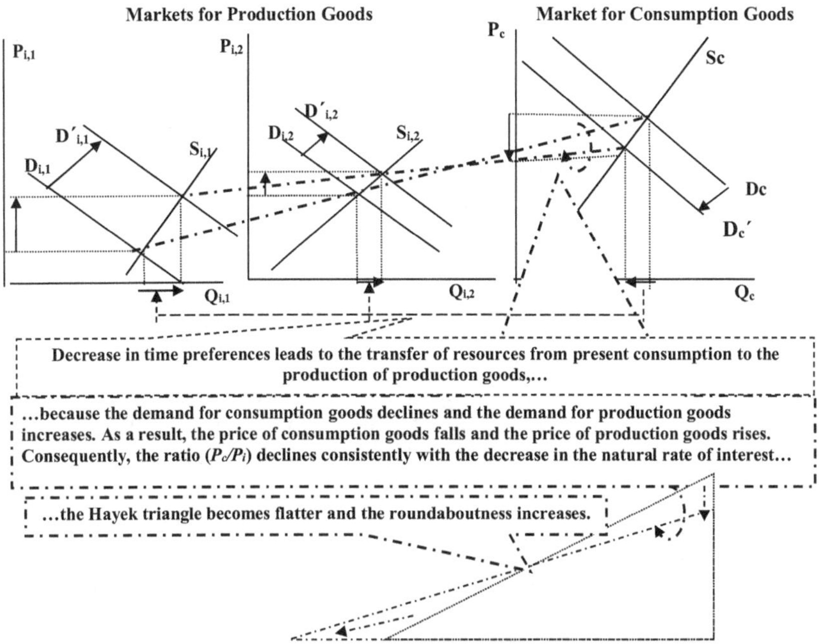

Fig. 4.2 Decrease in time preference and the structure of production

question is whether the economy is endowed with sufficient factors of production for supply to respond to higher demand, or whether the supply of production goods is fixed due to a lack of essential factors of production. There is no reason to believe that there was a considerable amount of free material resources or unemployed labour at the beginning of the processes. We therefore assume that the economy operates at its potential or full-employment level, where economic scarcity is a predominant feature. Analysis of an economy with idle resources and unemployed labour force appears in Chap. 8.

The answer to the aforementioned question can be found at the end of the production process, specifically in the consumption stage or in the stages very close to final consumption, which face reduced consumer demand. Lower demand will sooner or later cut consumer goods prices (P_c), as the right panel in Fig. 4.2 shows. Along with the inevitable reduction in their sales, lower prices will depress the profits of firms producing consumption goods. As a direct result, the factors of production at this stage will experience a fall in the value of their marginal product. In this way, the market manifests that, at the consumption stage, the factors of production are no longer valued as highly as before. The market therefore shows that, in the consumer goods sector, consumers value inputs more than the resulting output. Lower profits or even losses are an explicit signal that some factors of production should be released from this stage of the production process.[2]

As a result, the source of the factors of production, which are in high demand at earlier stages, can be found in the consumption stage. Figure 4.2 shows that the decrease in consumer demand should free up labour and other resources from this stage of the production process.[3] At the same time, higher demand for labour in the earlier stages can absorb it. If this reallocation occurs, the supply of consumption goods will fall, while the supply of production goods will rise. This process is conditioned on a well-functioning price system, which should reflect not only an increase in saving through a lower interest rate, but also a decline in consumption demand through a fall in consumer goods prices (P_c).[4] In addition, the price system must reflect the increase in demand for production goods by increasing their prices (P_i). The structure of wages in labour markets should be similarly affected. Earlier stages of production will experience

[2] Hayek (1932, p. 27), in a discussion with Keynes, added that, if entrepreneurs in the consumption stage continue to produce at an unchanged level, even when demand for their products decreases, the losses they suffer and the resulting decline in their capital can only be offset by reduction of their own consumption. However, this peculiar behaviour would block the release of factors of production from the consumption stage to the early stages, and production methods could never be lengthened.

[3] An interesting question is what will happen to consumption goods that are not sold due to falling consumer demand. Hayek (1941, p. 275) argued (in line with the simple story of Robinson Crusoe) that unless the goods in question deteriorate easily, they can wait in the stock of firms. They can then be used when the supply of consumption goods decreases due to the transfer of resources to the early stages, and when new longer processes have not yet provided finished consumption goods. At this particular moment, the stored consumer goods can be released from stock, alleviating their shortage in the market. At the same time, the opportunity costs of holding this stock are reduced due to the fall in the interest rate. Stocks of unsold goods are also discussed by Hicks ([1973] 1987).

[4] At this stage, we discuss the behaviour of the real part of the economy, which responded to changes in data transmitted through the price system. Potuzak (2018) shows the reaction of the economy if a decline in prices of consumption goods is not allowed (or not wanted) by the central bank.

wage growth, while stages closer to consumption experience decline, which is a direct signal for workers to move from one sector to another.

Several observations deserve attention. First, as can be seen in the market for loanable funds, both the natural and market interest rates have fallen. Second, the slope of the Hayek triangle becomes lower as demand for consumption goods decreases. The triangle is also longer, because a lower interest rate motivates entrepreneurs to increase the roundaboutness by opening new, longer production processes, which were unprofitable at a higher interest rate. This is consistent with the fact that the increase in demand for production goods is more robust in the production stages furthest from final consumption.[5]

Third, profit margins, represented by the difference in value between goods at different stages of production, are also lower, because there is a general tendency to equalize the profit rate with the interest rate. Fourth, although not immediately apparent from Fig. 4.2, capital in the economy has changed not only in size, but also in structure, as more factors of production are allocated to relatively more distant stages of production. In addition, some very early stages of production have been newly created.

As Hayek (1941, p. 78) pointed out, the (average) roundaboutness in the economy may be extended, even if no individual process as such has been lengthened. It is sufficient to release the necessary inputs from shorter processes (industries that operate closer to the consumption stage) and then absorb them in longer processes, in which production will increase. From a technical point of view, each industry follows the same line as before and uses the same methods. Nonetheless, the overall structure of production has changed, as more inputs are now invested in longer processes and in sectors further away from final consumption.

Processes in the labour market should be explained in more detail. It seems suspicious that the total demand for labour does not decrease as demand for consumption goods declines. Such reasoning would be perfectly consistent with the Marshallian theorem of derived demand. On the other hand, the classical statement of John Stuart Mill, which was studied in some detail by Hayek (1941, p. 436) in this context, argues that the demand for commodities is not the demand for labour.

[5] As shown in Fig. 4.2, there is a point in the structure of production at which demand neither rises nor falls. At this point, the so-called effect of derived demand and the time discount effect offset each other (Garrison, 2001).

Garrison (2001) developed an innovative approach that integrated both perspectives. Garrison argues that there are two effects throughout the production structure: the effect of derived demand and the time discount effect. The first pushes the demand for labour down as the demand for consumption goods declines. It is strong in the very late stages of production and in the final consumption stage. On the other hand, the time discount effect is affected by changes in the interest rate and is marked in the early stages of production, which are highly sensitive to the interest rate.

The idea of time discounting in factor markets, which was thoroughly elucidated by Hayek (1941) and Rothbard (2004), can be used to analyse labour markets at various stages of production. The demand for labour in every labour market depends on the marginal value product (MVP) of labour. However, in stages very far from final consumption, this value of the marginal product must be discounted at the prevailing interest rate, because the output of labour will only mature in consumer goods after a long time. The further a given stage is from final consumption, the more the given MVP is discounted.

Every profit-maximizing entrepreneur will hire workers to the point at which the discounted marginal value product (DMVP), not just the simple MVP, will equal the prevailing wage.[6] Market demand for labour must therefore depend on the DMVP rather than the MVP. The system of graphs in Fig. 4.3 illustrates this idea in detail. Curves in the MVP can be the same at all stages. However, markets differ in terms of the position of the DMVP. The further a given stage is from the final consumption, the lower its discounted marginal value product. Line AA, which connects the labour demand system and represents the time discount effect, is consistent with the slope of the Hayek triangle. In addition, if the labour force is non-specific and sufficiently mobile, an identical wage must prevail throughout the production structure (W_e).

The diagram in Fig. 4.3 can solve the puzzle mentioned by Block (1990). The different discounted marginal value product at various stages of the production structure seems to contradict the assumption of identical wages that result from arbitrage across labour markets. However, the

[6] The formula for the discounted marginal value product of labour is: $DMVP = MVP/(1 + i)^t = (P_c \cdot MPL)/(1 + i)^t$, where P_c is the price of the final consumable output, MPL is the physical marginal product of labour, i is the interest rate, and t is the time required for the process to mature.

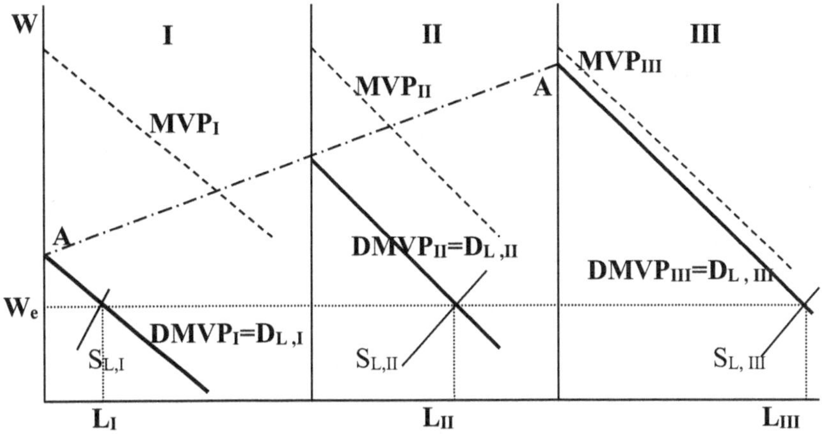

Fig. 4.3 Labour markets in various stages of the structure of production

DMVP depends not only on the size of the time discount and the position of the MVP, but also on the amount of labour hired. As a result of the diminishing physical marginal product of labour (MPL), the MVP and DMVP fall with more employed workers. It is therefore necessary to distinguish the position of the entire DMVP curve and one specific point on this curve. Mobility of workers will ensure that the DMVP and wages are identical at all stages of the production process, even though the position of the DMVP curves differs.

Suppose that people start saving more. This will reduce the demand for present consumption goods and decrease both natural and market interest rates. As demonstrated earlier, the price of consumption goods declines, which must reduce the marginal value product (MVP) of labour. However, the impact on the discounted marginal product of labour (DMVP), which is crucial for labour demand in every market, is ambiguous. As shown in Fig. 4.4, the DMVP declines in stages close to final consumption (right panel), and rises in stages in which the MVP is significantly discounted (left panel). In the first case, the effect of derived demand dominates the time discount effect, because the decrease in the interest rate is not strong enough to compensate for the decline in the MVP. However, in stages very far from final consumption, the time discount effect is crucial, which leads to the DMVP moving in the opposite direction to the MVP.

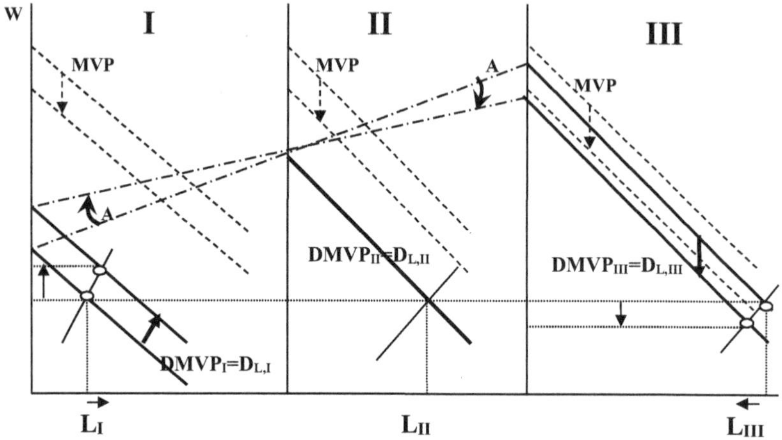

Fig. 4.4 Labour markets in various stages of the structure of production—decrease in time preference

The slope of line AA falls, demonstrating a lower rate of interest. The decline in demand for consumption goods has an ambiguous effect on the demand for labour. Labour demand decreases in stages close to final consumption (right panel), but increases in the early stages (left panel), which produce capital goods of various forms that mature into final consumption goods in the distant future. The same movement applies to wages, which increase in the early stages and decline in the later stages.

As shown in Fig. 4.4, there is one particular stage in which the effect of derived demand is perfectly offset by the time discount effect.[7] Its exact position can be identified with a simple present value model:

$$\text{DMVP} = \frac{\text{MVP}}{(1+i)^t} = \frac{P_c.\text{MPL}}{(1+i)^t} \tag{4.1}$$

P_c is the price of the final consumption good, MPL is the physical marginal product of labour, i is the interest rate, and t is the time required for the process to mature. The decline in consumption demand reduces the price P_c, but also the interest rate i. It is clear that the longer it takes for a

[7] See also the discussion in O'Driscoll and Rizzo (1996, p. 205).

given project to mature into final consumption goods (higher t), the more important the effect of the interest rate on the DMVP is compared to the effect of the price. The specific t, for which both effects compensate each other, can be derived as follows.

The total differential of the DMVP is given by:

$$d\text{DMVP} = \frac{\partial \text{DMVP}}{\partial P_c} dP_c + \frac{\partial \text{DMVP}}{\partial MPL} d\text{MPL} + \frac{\partial \text{DMVP}}{\partial i} di \tag{4.2}$$

Assuming zero change in the physical marginal product of labour (dMPL = 0), Eq. (4.2) leads to:

$$d\text{DMVP} = \frac{\partial \text{DMVP}}{\partial P_c} dP_c + \frac{\partial \text{DMVP}}{\partial i} di \tag{4.3}$$

$$d\text{DMVP} = \frac{\text{MPL}}{(1+i)^t} dP_c - t\frac{P_c \cdot \text{MPL}}{(1+i)^{t+1}} di \tag{4.4}$$

Both effects compensate each other if the change in the DMVP is zero:

$$d\text{DMVP} = 0 \tag{4.5}$$

$$0 = \frac{\text{MPL}}{(1+i)^t} dP_c - t\frac{P_c \cdot \text{MPL}}{(1+i)^{t+1}} di \tag{4.6}$$

$$t\frac{P_c \cdot \text{MPL}}{(1+i)^{t+1}} di = \frac{\text{MPL}}{(1+i)^t} dP_c \tag{4.7}$$

$$t = \frac{dP_c}{P_c} \frac{1+i}{di} \tag{4.8}$$

For example, if the initial interest rate was i = 5% per year and declined by one percentage point (di = -1%), and if the price of the final consumption goods was reduced by 5% (dP_c/P_c = -5%), then a straightforward calculation shows that t = 5.25 years. As a result, projects that mature in 5 years or more will benefit from increased savings. From this stage to the early stages, the demand for labour will increase.

If the labour force is sufficiently mobile and non-specific, the situation in Fig. 4.4 is not sustainable. The wage gap between different markets will attract the labour force to the early stages and motivate workers to leave the stages close to final consumption. This mechanism will therefore reallocate the labour force into longer processes and allow the production structure to be lengthened.

The final picture of the economy is illustrated in Fig. 4.5, which depicts the new equilibrium. Stages far from final consumption attracted more of the labour force (left panel) at the expense of later stages (right panel). Some workers may even have found jobs in very roundabout processes that were newly created due to the decrease in the interest rate (Garrison, 2001).[8]

Labour reallocation ends when wages are identical in all markets. The final level of this nominal wage is difficult to determine. The height of the Hayek triangle is lower, so the nominal value of the product from which wages can be paid is reduced (Rothbard, 2004). On the other hand, the interest rate is also lower, so the part of the output that can be attributed to workers is higher (Hayek, 1935a). These two effects work against each

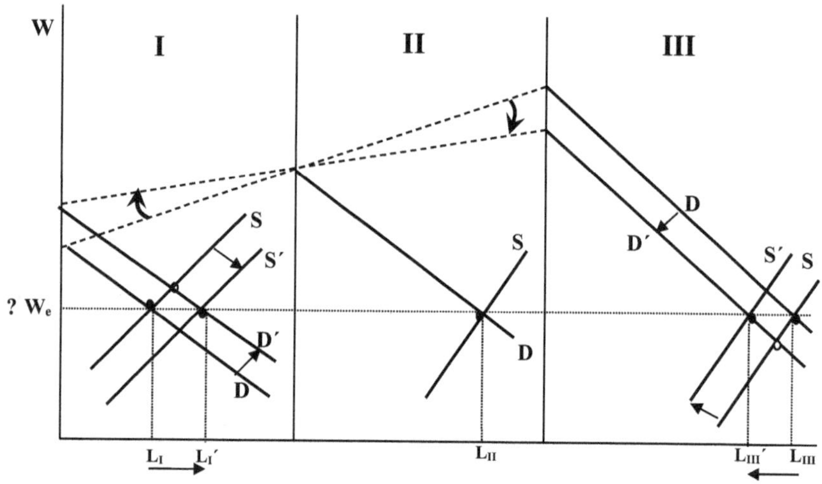

Fig. 4.5 Final equilibrium in the labour markets

[8] All features of the process analysed apply to any factor of production and can easily be generalized to circulating capital.

other. As a result, the final level of the nominal wage cannot be determined using this model.

The more important issue is the size of the real wage. Because prices of consumption goods declined, the real wage could increase. However, we are interested in the size of the real wage when the new, longer processes are completed, and when they start to provide finished consumer goods. To address this, we develop a model based on Fig. 2.1 in Chap. 2, with two methods of specific length. This figure will not only compare the productivity of two different processes, but also clarify the behaviour of the economy during the transition period.

Suppose that the economy is endowed with five units of labour and uses only direct methods. Every labourer produces one unit of output after one period. As shown in Fig. 4.6, at time $t - 1$, the total amount of consumption goods in this economy is five. Restructuring into longer processes begins at time t. We assume that the labour force will gradually be transferred to longer methods. At time t, one unit of labour is allocated to a process that will mature in five periods, that is, to the roundabout process illustrated in panel (b) of Fig. 2.1.

At time t, the output of consumption goods falls to four units, because only four direct processes provide consumption goods. At time $t + 1$, another unit of labour is devoted to the roundabout method, and the total output of final consumption goods declines to three. Three units of labour produce consumption goods in direct processes, one unit of labour works on intermediate product II, and one worker processes intermediate product I.

At time $t + 2$, $t + 3$, and $t + 4$, the remaining units of labour are allocated to long processes, and the output of consumer goods gradually falls to its minimum at time $t + 3$. The cause of this decline has already been discussed and can be read from the picture. The labour force has been diverted from processes that provide consumption goods directly, so their production decreases. In addition, the longer and more productive processes to which workers have been allocated do not yet produce final consumption goods. These methods are not yet mature.

However, Fig. 4.6 characterizes only production, not consumption. In a given period, total consumption may differ from the total production of consumer goods. For example, actual consumption in the transition period can be higher than actual production if a sufficient amount of consumer goods was saved before the start of the transformation. After all, it was the

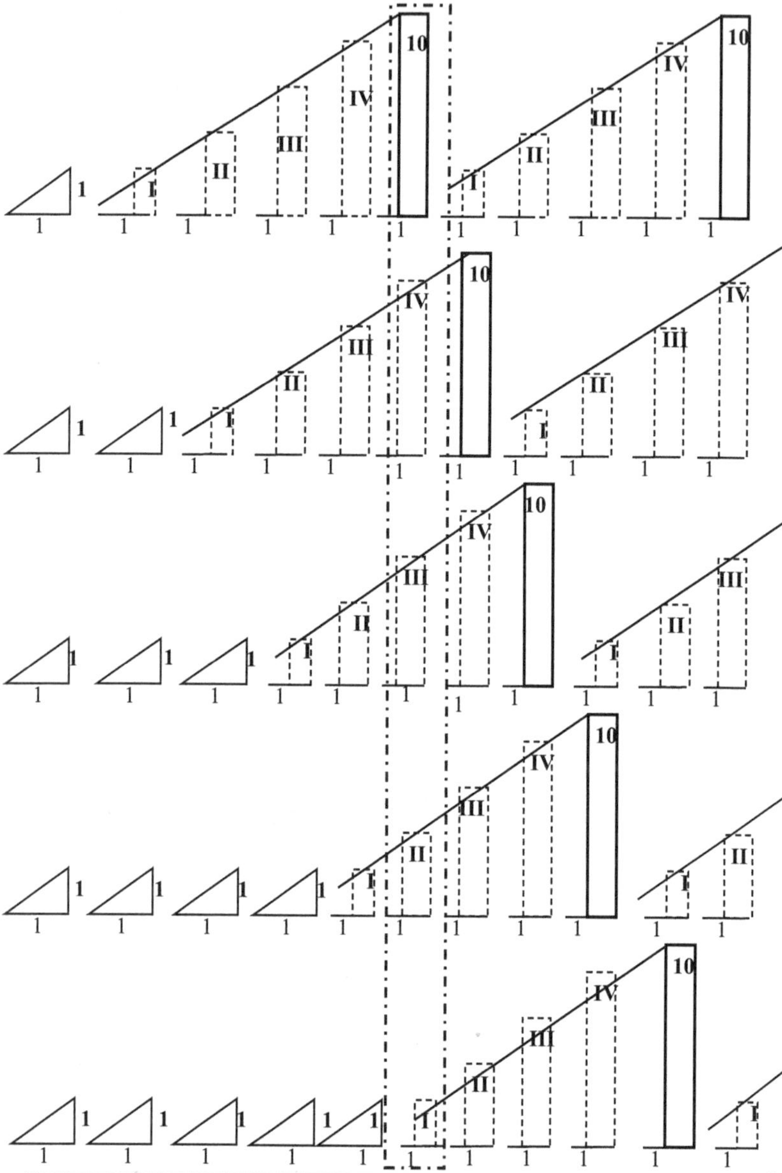

Fig. 4.6 Gradual restructuring of production processes

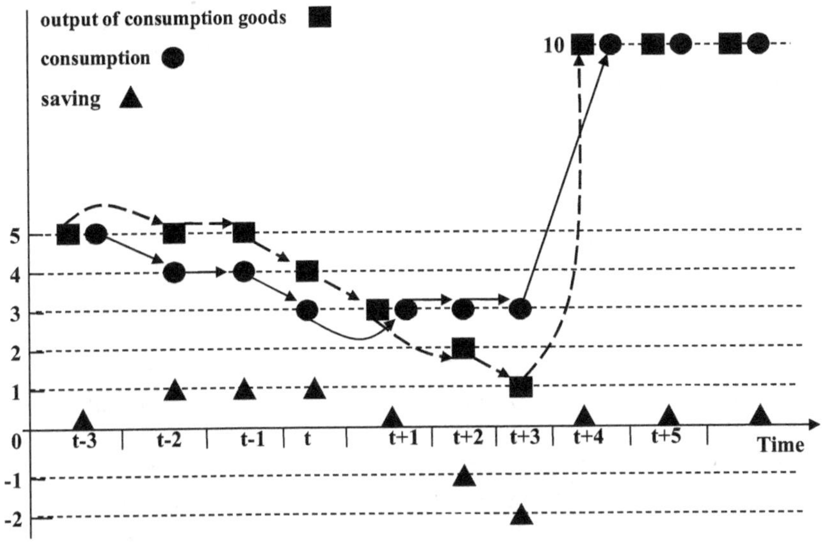

Fig. 4.7 Evolution of the production of consumer goods, consumption, and saving

reduction in consumption demand that initiated the lengthening of the production process.

One possible consumption path is shown in Fig. 4.7. Demand for present consumer goods decreases in period $t - 2$, that is, two periods before the start of the restructuring of production methods. Consumption is below actual output for three periods (from $t - 2$ to t). Three units of consumption goods are gradually accumulated and subsequently used in periods of minimum production ($t + 2$ and $t + 3$). This picture also retains the assumption of reasonable consumption smoothing. Hayek's (1941) description of unsold consumption goods that can be used when the process is in transition seems quite plausible.

Figures 4.6 and 4.7 show that, at time $t + 4$, the first roundabout process provides final consumption goods, and total output rises from one to ten. Higher output and consumption can be maintained in the following periods as other processes gradually mature. Increased demand for future consumption goods, which was reflected in higher saving in the past, is eventually met by a greater supply of these goods. According to Austrian theory, the price system delivers information from consumers to entrepreneurs. It can shape the production structure accordingly, so that the production plans of firms are consistent with the intertemporal preferences of consumers.

In the end, only a fifth of the total labour force is devoted to the production of final consumption goods. Initially, it was 100%. However, in short processes, the total output of consumption goods was lower than in the long process. At the aggregate level, five workers produced five units using short methods, while after the transformation, ten units are produced using long processes. In effect, one unit of output per unit of labour was produced with the short method, while two units per worker are now produced using the long method.

After lengthening the production methods, a greater proportion of the labour force is devoted to producing various forms of intermediate products I, II, III, IV, which will mature into consumption goods at different times in the future.[9] In addition, most of the "wealth" in the economy is in the form of work-in-progress than in final consumption goods.

The cross-sectional picture of the economy at time $t + 4$ in Fig. 4.6 can easily confuse sound reasoning. It seems as if the output of consumption goods was produced in a single period out of intermediate products I, II, III, IV. However, the complex picture in Fig. 4.6 clearly proves that the Knightian idea of synchronous production is illusory. The production of final consumption goods using the roundabout method takes five periods, not one. The phenomenon of time is therefore of the utmost importance in production analysis and capital theory.[10]

From time $t + 4$, the output of consumption goods will be permanently greater. This allows us to answer the question about the size of the real wage. Real wages should definitely be higher than before the transformation to roundabout processes. In the neoclassical model, accumulation of capital raises the marginal product of labour, which should be reflected in higher real wages in competitive markets. According to Austrian capital theory, this phenomenon arises due to the higher productivity of roundabout methods.

[9] It can be argued that a given worker will only specialize in the production of one particular intermediate good, for example, III. This specialization and the vertical division of labour noted above can further increase the productivity of the longer process.

[10] Compare this theory with the Knightian approach in Knight (1934, 1935a, 1935b, 1936a, 1936b). The Hayek perspective can be also found in Hayek (1935b, 1936a, 1936b).

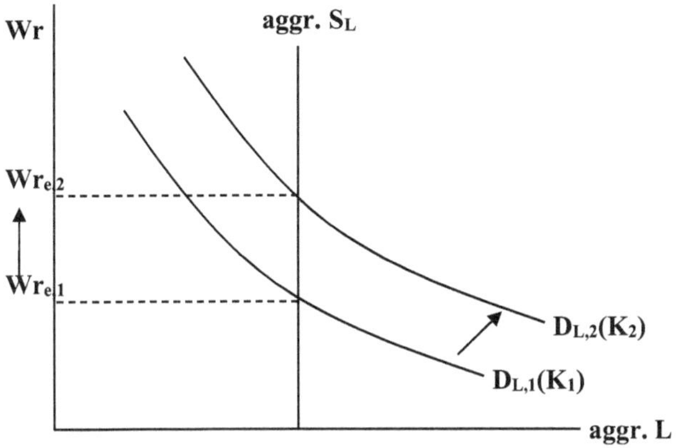

Fig. 4.8 Increase in capital and the aggregate labour market

The Austrian approach can be compared with the standard neoclassical labour market model. Neoclassical labour economics uses an aggregative model, such as the one depicted in Fig. 4.8. For simplicity, the labour supply is sketched as a vertical line. The demand for labour shifts outwards because there is higher capital stock in the economy, which increases the marginal product of labour. The equilibrium real wage grows from $Wr_{e,1}$ to $Wr_{e,2}$.

The neoclassical approach seems rather sterile when examining the fundamental processes of labour force reallocation analysed earlier. The total quantity of labour remains the same, and the real wage rises. To develop a more precise insight, this aggregative approach might be replaced with a more detailed analysis proposed in Figs. 4.3, 4.4, and 4.5, which investigate separate labour markets at different stages of the production process. Otherwise, the essential insight could be lost in aggregation.

We can conclude that the reduction in consumption demand and the resulting higher saving eventually benefit workers. However, the entire process is more complex than is usually illustrated in textbook growth models, as shown below. The essence of the act of saving is that the factors of production are partly diverted from producing final consumption goods and are devoted to longer processes, which will lead to more consumer goods, though after a longer period of time.

In this context, Böhm-Bawerk (1891, p. 101) raised the question whether the source of capital accumulation was saving or production. The

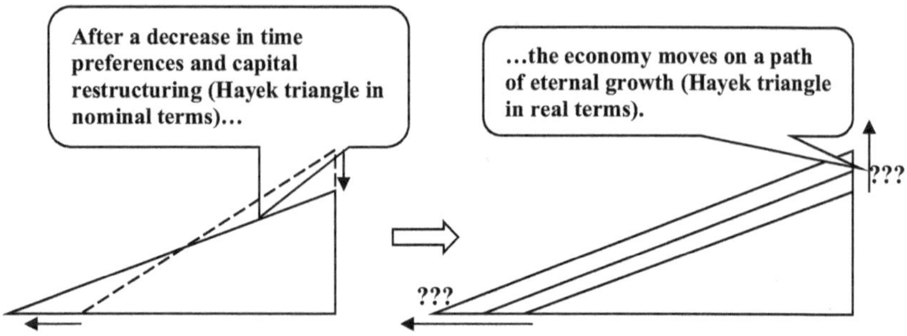

Fig. 4.9 Possible eternal growth after a decrease in time preferences

foregoing analysis demonstrated that Böhm-Bawerk was correct in saying that both were. Factors of production must first be saved, that is, not used in shorter processes, and then must be devoted to longer production processes that mature after a longer time period. The act of saving necessarily requires extending the time for which the particular factors of production are used in the production process (Hayek, 1941). The role of consumption goods in the act of saving that Jevons (1957) emphasized, and which is stressed even in modern economics, is that reduction of demand for final consumption goods and their possible accumulation can bridge the transition period during which production methods are being restructured. In this respect, theories such as neoclassical growth models, which assume that saved consumption goods will immediately transform into capital goods, are rather naïve. This easy transformation may only hold for an insignificant part of the entire capital stock. In most cases, capital goods must be newly created using factors of production released from shorter processes.

The final critical issue associated with a change in time preference is the evolution of the economy after the production process has been restructured to longer methods. Garrison (2001, p. 64) examined this question in some detail and predicted that, after the reduction in time preference, the economy could move forward on a path of never-ending (secular) growth (or higher growth rate) of the output of consumption goods. This trajectory is illustrated in Fig. 4.9.[11]

[11] It might be argued that Garrison's approach is quite inconsistent, because it does not distinguish between Hayekian triangles in nominal and real terms. When it is inevitable for clarity of exposition, we will explicitly discuss whether the figure is in nominal terms or in real terms, as in Fig. 4.9.

However, Fig. 4.9 features question marks, because such a result seems highly unlikely, especially if we again consider assumptions about capital. We may ask whether the increase in the level of output will be permanent, so the rising growth rate is only temporary and gradually approaches zero. We can question whether the increase in the growth rate will be permanent, as Garrison suggests, which will result in an indefinite increase in the level of output. The last option is that the level of output will increase only temporarily and then return to its previous level.

Figures 4.6 and 4.7 suggest that a higher output of ten units is sustainable if the necessary amount of labour is constantly devoted to longer processes. It will remain at this constant level, which cannot increase steadily, as Garrison assumed. If part of the labour force (e.g. 1 unit) reverts to a shorter process, output will increase to 11 units in response to this change and stay at 11 units in the following three periods. In the fourth period, the output will suddenly drop to one unit.[12] If the total labour force is permanently allocated to longer processes, which means that the saving rate remains the same as in periods of transition to roundabout methods, the output may be sustainable at a higher level of ten units. However, this level will not increase unless consumers further reduce their time preference and increase the saving rate.

Higher incomes lead to both higher consumption and saving, and thus larger amounts of capital. A greater level of output can therefore be maintained. A higher saving rate must be preserved, as must the necessary investment to keep the larger stock of capital intact, that is, to maintain the longer methods of production undisturbed.

If the assumption of diminishing marginal productivity of roundabout methods is met, it is unlikely that economic growth could be eternal, as Garrison (2001) argued. In other words, a diminishing marginal product of capital implies that every additional unit of capital is less productive. Thus, after an increase in the saving rate, it is impossible for the consumer goods output to grow steadily at a constant rate, rather than a declining rate. Salerno (2001), in his critique of Garrison's approach, stated that only a permanently decreasing time preference can lead to ever-increasing output. This conclusion appears to be consistent with the predictions of standard growth models, as shown below.

[12] In this scheme, when four processes are roundabout and one is direct, the sequence of output is as follows: 1, 11, 11, 11, 11; 1, 11, 11, 11, 11; 1, 11, 11, 11, 11...

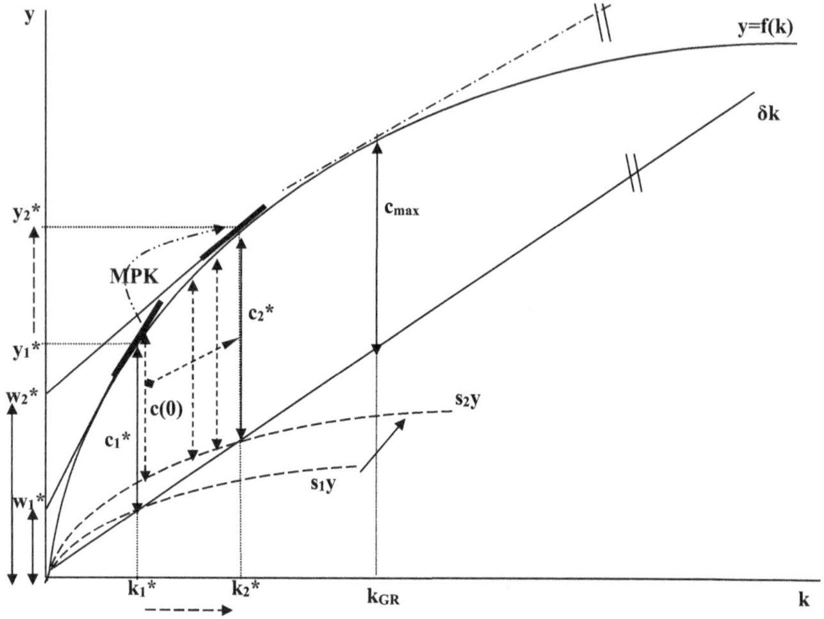

Fig. 4.10 Impossibility of eternal growth in the Solow model

Consider a Solow (1956) growth model with a stationary population and constant technology. The growth rate of the labour force is therefore zero ($n = 0$), as is the growth rate of the labour augmenting technological progress ($g = 0$). In this neoclassical framework, capital goods and consumption goods are of the same type. It is a simple single-commodity model. Saved consumption goods are immediately converted into capital goods. In contrast to the Austrian model, the processes of capital restructuring and its creation may be hidden in aggregation.[13]

Point k_1^* in Fig. 4.10 represents the steady state of capital per worker ($k = K/L$), at which the depreciated capital (δk) is completely replaced,

[13]The Solow model with homogenous capital and aggregate production function is applied for pedagogical reasons. The Austrian approach to this model can be found, for example, in Lewin (1999), and Lewin and Cachanosky (2019b). In addition, Cambridge capital controversies (Samuelson, 1966) are ignored in our simple model. For the Austrian perspective, the interested reader is referred to Rosser (2020), Fratini (2019), and Lewin and Cachanosky (2019a).

thanks to new saving and investment (s_1y). Depreciation of capital is thus equal to gross investment (and saving), $\delta k_1^* = s_1 y_1^*$, where $y_1^* = f(k_1^*)$, and net investment is zero, $\Delta k_1^* = 0$. The steady state consumption c_1^* is sustainable and stable. If consumers permanently increase their saving rate from s_1 to s_2, consumption drops to $c(0)$ and capital accumulation begins. The economy is starting to grow. However, due to the positive ($MPK = f'(k) > 0$), but diminishing, marginal product of capital ($f''(k) < 0$), the higher saving rate as a source of growth is gradually being exhausted. Eventually, the economy finds a new steady state with higher capital per worker (k_2^*), output per worker[14] (y_2^*), and consumption per worker (c_2^*).[15] The real rate of interest r will decline due to the decrease in the marginal product of capital, where $r_2^* = [f'(k_2^*) - \delta] < r_1^* = [f'(k_1^*) - \delta]$. This model also shows that the final real wage w_2^* exceeds the initial level w_1^* (Barro, 2004, p. 41).[16]

Garrison's prediction of eternal (or secular) growth is therefore unattainable if the marginal product of capital is diminishing, the population (labour force) is stationary, and technological progress is zero. The Solow model can produce indefinite growth of output per worker only with a positive growth rate of technological progress ($g > 0$). The economy can then be on a balanced growth path (BGP). Eternal growth is also possible in models with a constant marginal product of capital, a feature known from the AK models of the new growth theory.

Salerno (2001) was correct that only constantly declining time preferences (a permanently increasing saving rate in the Solow model) can create eternal growth. This scenario is not completely ruled out if the rate of impatience (time preference) decreases as average income rises (Fisher, 1930). However, with regard to the predictions of the Solow model, there

[14] In the Solow model, output represents the total amount of final goods (one type of good produced in the economy), which is either devoted to consumption or investment. It is also equal to the total income that can be used for consumption or saving. Saving is equal to investment in this model in each period t.

[15] Consumption will eventually be higher only if the economy is dynamically efficient (Phelps, 1961, 1965). As illustrated in Fig. 4.10, the steady state level of capital k^* must be below the golden rule level k_{GR}, where consumption is maximized at the steady state c_{MAX}. Assuming a stationary population and technology ($n = g = 0$), the golden rule level of capital is a point where the real rate of interest is zero $r_{GR} = 0$. In Fig. 4.10, it can be indicated at the point where the slope of the production function equals the slope of the depreciation curve, $f'(k_{GR}) = \delta$.

[16] This inverse relationship between the real interest rate and the real wage is analysed by Hicks (1987).

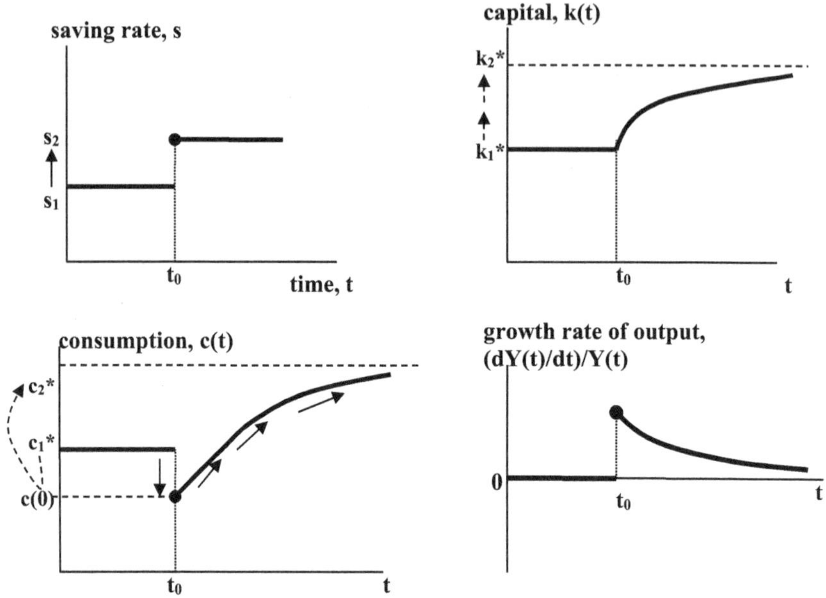

Fig. 4.11 The evolution of the key variables after an increase in the saving rate

is a limit to the level of consumption that can be permanently achieved with an ever-increasing saving rate. This limit is the well-known golden rule level of capital accumulation (Phelps, 1961, 1965), where steady-state consumption is maximized. Above this level, the economy over-accumulates capital, and a decrease in time preferences (increase in the saving rate) is no longer beneficial for steady-state consumption.

The evolution of the key variables is outlined in Fig. 4.11.[17] The saving rate permanently rises from s_1 to s_2 at time t_0. Capital per worker is gradually accumulated from k_1^* to k_2^*. The picture of the real wage and output per worker in the transition process closely resembles the evolution of capital per worker. Consumption per worker drops from c_1^* to $c(0)$ at time t_0, as the saving rate increases. This is followed by continuous growth in consumption to a new higher level c_2^*. The new level of consumption is greater than the initial level if the economy is dynamically efficient. The

[17] This system of graphs appears in Romer (2006, p. 19, p. 66).

lower right panel shows that the growth rate of output is temporarily supported. However, due to the diminishing marginal product of capital, the effect of this stimulus is gradually declining.

For the evolution of the natural rate of interest, we use the Ramsay-Cass-Koopmans model. The idea of lower time preference in this model is presented as a decrease in the subjective discount rate ρ, which shifts the consumption locus in Fig. 4.12 to the right.[18] The qualitative characteristics of the other key variables are very similar to those of the Solow model. With the accumulation of capital, the natural rate of interest $r(t)$ gradually falls from r_1^* to r_2^*, which equals the new level of the subjective discount rate ρ_2.[19]

These neoclassical models shed some light on the processes of capital accumulation and the evolution of consumption over time. However, because they rely on the assumption of homogenous capital, some important issues may be hidden. In Austrian capital theory, the accumulation of capital, triggered by a reduction in consumption demand, is accompanied by a change in the capital structure (Lachmann, 1978). This process also requires reallocation of the labour force to longer methods. In this particular respect, the neoclassical models are silent.

Imbalance in the Capital Structure

Interest rate movements have been shown to reflect changes in real factors on the market, which ensures its smooth functioning. Another issue is whether the interest rate can clear the market when an imbalance in the intertemporal structure of production arises.

Suppose that the market interest rate is below the equilibrium level ($r_2 < r_E$), as in Fig. 4.13. This results in an excess of supply over demand

[18] Ramsey (1928) did not accept the idea of underestimation of future wants and did not include the subjective discount rate in his model. In order to avoid the divergence of the utility integral with increasing output and consumption, he assumed the satiation of wants sometime in the future at the so-called bliss point. Cass (1965) and Koopmans (1963) introduced the subjective discount rate into the model.

[19] It can be demonstrated that the formula for the steady-state real rate of interest is $r^* = \rho + \theta g$ (Romer, 2006), where $1/\theta$ is the intertemporal elasticity of substitution in consumption. Figure 4.11 assumes constant technology ($g = 0\%$). The steady-state real rate of interest is then determined solely by the subjective discount rate ρ (pure time preference). It can be shown that, in the convergence period, the interest rate also depends on the marginal product of capital. This conclusion is in line with Hayek's (1941) insights.

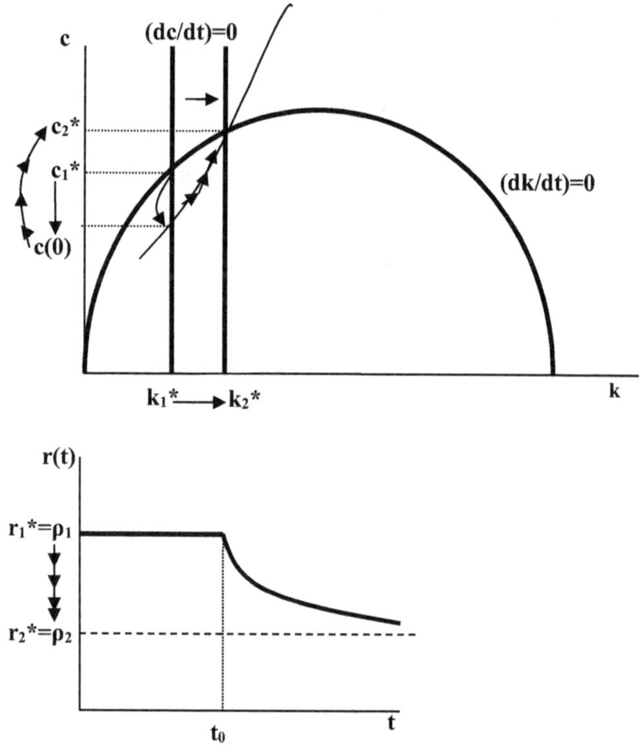

Fig. 4.12 The evolution of the economy after a decrease in impatience in the RCK model

in the markets for production goods ($S_i > D_i$). In contrast, consumer goods markets suffer from a shortage of supply ($S_c < D_c$). If the price system works efficiently, prices of production goods should decline, with a more pronounced fall in the earliest stages of production, while prices of consumption goods should rise. The price ratio between consumption and production goods (P_c/P_i) will increase, in line with the fact that the interest rate on the loanable funds market is rising, and gradually equilibrates saving and investment. As Fig. 4.13 shows, the response of the price system eliminates the initial imbalances in both the structure of production and the loanable funds market. Resources are reallocated to remove excess supply or demand.

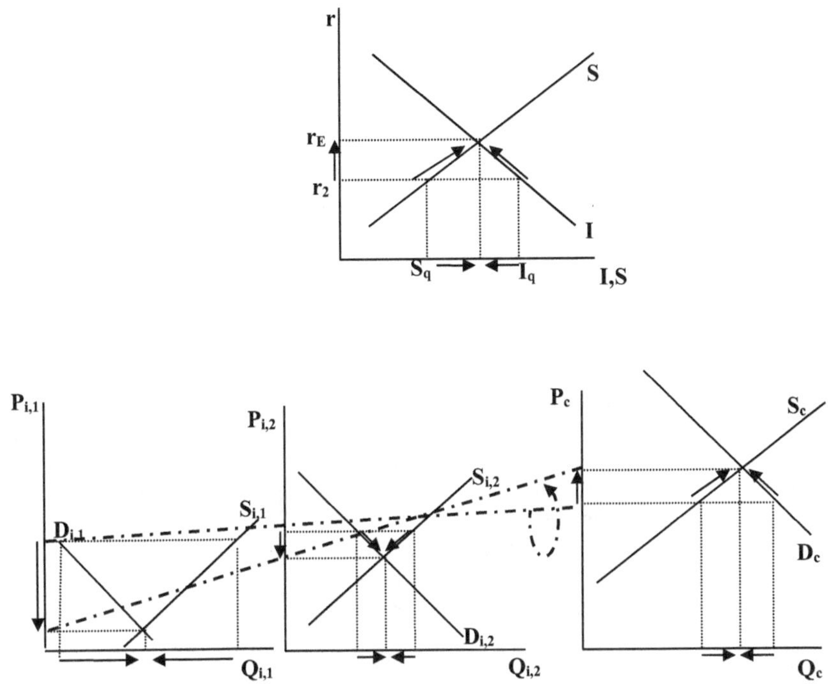

Fig. 4.13 Imbalance in the structure of production gradually eliminated by the price movements

According to Austrian theory, the role of the interest rate should not be underestimated, as it guides the entire process of capital restructuring. It mirrors the slope of the system of demand functions at different stages of the production process and eventually decides which of these stages will be newly created, expand, contract, or disappear altogether. Hayek wrote in this context:

> *But to think of interest only as a direct cost factor is to overlook its main influence on production. What is much more important is its effect on prices through its effect on demand for the intermediate products and for the factors from which they are produced.*
>
> Hayek (1935a, p. 83)

The prior analysis suggests that the interest rate transmits key information about the changes in the intertemporal markets. It represents a guideline in a market economy, as to how scarce resources should optimally be allocated over time to maximize utility and profit. If this signal is distorted for reasons that do not stem from the real economy, this is unlikely to have a null effect on the intertemporal allocation of resources. The key question is whether the sequence of events thus triggered is sustainable or whether the process initiated by non-real (e.g. monetary) factors will eventually reverse.

References

Barro, R. J. (2004). *Economic Growth* (2nd ed.). MIT Press.

Block, W. (1990). The DMVP-MVP Controversy: A Note. *The Review of Austrian Economics, 4*(1), 199–207.

Cass, D. (1965). Optimum Growth in an Aggregative Model of Capital Accumulation. *Review of Economic Studies, 37*(3), 233–240.

Fisher, I. (1930). *Theory of Interest.* The Macmillan Company.

Fratini, S. M. (2019). A Note on Re-switching, the Average Period of Production and the Austrian Business-Cycle Theory. *The Review of Austrian Economics, 32*, 363–374.

Garrison, R. W. (2001). *Time and Money, The Macroeconomics of Capital Structure.* Routledge.

Hicks, J. R. (1987 [1973]). *Capital and Time: A Neo-Austrian Theory.* Oxford University Press.

Jevons, W. S. (1957 [1871]). *The Theory of Political Economy.* Sentry Press.

Knight, F. H. (1934). Capital, Time, and the Interest Rate. *Economica, 1*(3), 257–286.

Knight, F. H. (1935a). Professor Hayek and the Theory of Investment. *The Economic Journal, 45*(177), 77–94.

Knight, F. H. (1935b). The Theory of Investment Once More: Mr. Boulding and the Austrians. *The Quarterly Journal of Economics, 50*(1), 36–67.

Knight, F. H. (1936a). The Quantity of Capital and the Rate of Interest: I. *The Journal of Political Economy, 44*(4), 433–463.

Knight, F. H. (1936b). The Quantity of Capital and the Rate of Interest: II. *The Journal of Political Economy, 44*(5), 612–642.

Koopmans, T. C. (1963). *On the Concept of Optimal Economic Growth.* Cowles Foundation Discussion Papers 163, Cowles Foundation for Research in Economics, Yale University.

Lachmann, L. M. (1978 [1956]). *Capital and Its Structure.* Institute for Humane Studies.

Lewin, P. (1999). *Capital in Disequilibrium: The Role of Capital in a Changing World*. Routledge.
Lewin, P., & Cachanosky, N. (2019a). Re-switching, the Average Period of Production and the Austrian Business-Cycle Theory: A Comment on Fratini. *The Review of Austrian Economics, 32*, 375–382.
Lewin, P., & Cachanosky, N. (2019b). *Austrian Capital Theory: A Modern Survey of the Essentials*. Cambridge University Press.
O'Driscoll, G. P., Jr., & Rizzo, M. J. (1996). *The Economics of Time and Ignorance* (2nd ed.). Routledge.
Phelps, E. S. (1961). The Golden Rule of Accumulation: A Fable for Growthmen. *The American Economic Review, 51*(4), 638–643.
Phelps, E. S. (1965). Second Essay on the Golden Rule of Accumulation. *The American Economic Review, 55*(4), 793–814.
Potuzak, P. (2018). Price Level Stabilization: Hayek Contra Mainstream Economics. *Prague Economic Papers, 27*(4), 449–478.
Potuzak, P. (2021). Demand for Money and Hayekian Triangles. *Revista Procesos De Mercado, 18*(1), 299–317.
Ramsey, F. P. (1928). A Mathematical Theory of Saving. *Economic Journal, 38*(152), 543–559.
Romer, D. (2006). *Advanced Macroeconomics* (3rd ed.). McGraw-Hill.
Rosser, J. B. (2020). Austrian Themes and the Cambridge Capital Theory Controversies. *The Review of Austrian Economics, 33*, 415–431.
Rothbard, M. N. (2004 [1962]). *Man, Economy, and State*. Ludwig von Mises Institute.
Salerno, J. T. (2001). Does the Concept of Secular Growth Have a Place in Capital-Based Macroeconomics? *The Quarterly Journal of Austrian Economics, 4*(3), 43–61.
Samuelson, P. A. (1966). A Summing Up. *The Quarterly Journal of Economics, 80*(4), 568–583.
Solow, R. M. (1956). A Contribution to the Theory of Economic Growth. *The Quarterly Journal of Economics, 70*(1), 65–94.
von Böhm-Bawerk, E. (1891 [1888]). *Positive Theory of Capital*. G. E. Stechert.
von Hayek, F. A. (1932). Reflections on the Pure Theory of Money of Mr. J. M. Keynes (Continued). *Economica, 35*, 22–44.
von Hayek, F. A. (1935a [1931]). *Prices and Production* (2nd ed.). Augustus M. Kelly.
von Hayek, F. A. (1935b). The Maintenance of Capital. *Economica, 2*(7), 241–276.
von Hayek, F. A. (1936a). The Mythology of Capital. *Quarterly Journal of Economics, 50*(2), 199–228.
von Hayek, F. A. (1936b). Utility Analysis and Interest. *The Economic Journal, 46*(181), 44–60.
von Hayek, F. A. (1941). *The Pure Theory of Capital*. The University of Chicago Press.

PART II

Austrian Business Cycle Theory

CHAPTER 5

Austrian Business Cycle Theory: A Basic Model

Austrian business cycle theory stands and falls on the Austrian theory of capital. In this chapter, the graphical apparatus developed in the previous chapters is used to elucidate Austrian business cycle theory.

Although the interest rate was introduced as a variable that brings equilibrium to real phenomena, that is, saving and investment in the loanable funds market, neither investment nor saving is traded in kind in the real world. Flows of saving and investment come to the market in the form of money. As a result, it is sometimes difficult to identify a certain exchange as an act of saving or of investment. Moreover, it is inconceivable that a change in the monetary sector, that is, the money supply or demand for money, will not affect the market for loanable funds. Only in a hypothetical barter economy, where investment equals saving by definition, would problems such as those discussed in this chapter not arise.

One of the most important disturbances that the loanable funds market may face from the monetary side of the economy is a change in the money supply. Assume that the central bank injects a certain amount of a generally accepted medium of exchange into the money market. Using any tool at its disposal, this money should end up as new reserves in commercial banks. Although it is conceivable that the story will end here, in normal times the optimal ratio of reserves to deposits in commercial banks is somewhat disturbed, which motivates them to re-establish a more profitable relationship. Their straightforward response is usually to offer their clients, whether old or new, more loans.

P. Potuzak, *Austrian Theory of Capital and Business Cycle*,
https://doi.org/10.1007/978-3-031-18728-5_5

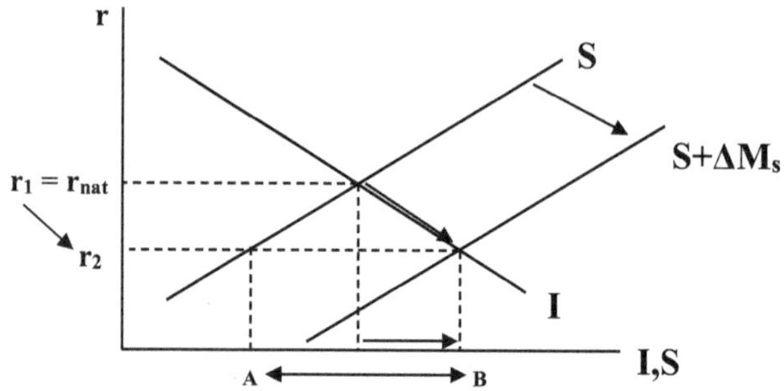

Fig. 5.1 Monetary expansion in the loanable funds market

This action will increase the supply of loanable funds in the market (Garrison, 2001). Assuming a stable investment demand function, new loans will only be accepted at a lower interest rate. Monetary expansion will therefore lead to an overall decrease in market interest rates.[1] As Fig. 5.1 shows, the interest rate in the loanable funds market falls below the natural rate ($r_2 < r_{nat}$). The real forces determining the natural level have not changed. For some time, monetary expansion may create a negative gap between the actual market interest rate and the natural rate (O'Driscoll & Rizzo, 1996, p. 203).

Although the natural rate of interest does not change at this stage of the process, information about the scarcity of factors of production and the relative demand for present and future consumption goods is conveyed by the lowered market interest rate ($r_2 < r_1$). The decline in the market interest rate is an explicit signal to producers that demand for production goods has increased, at the expense of demand for consumption goods. The net present value of projects that are highly sensitive to the interest rate becomes positive. The strongest response can be expected for processes that will mature at a relatively distant point in time in the future. As a result, profitable opportunities to produce more capital goods emerge, in addition to opportunities to open new stages of production processes that would never have been lucrative if the interest rate had not declined.

Economic agents cannot recognize that the decrease in the interest rate was caused by the expansion of the money supply rather than by an increase

[1] In a critique of the Banking School theories, Mises ([1912] 2009) clarified that virtually any amount of newly created money can be placed on the market by reducing interest rates sufficiently.

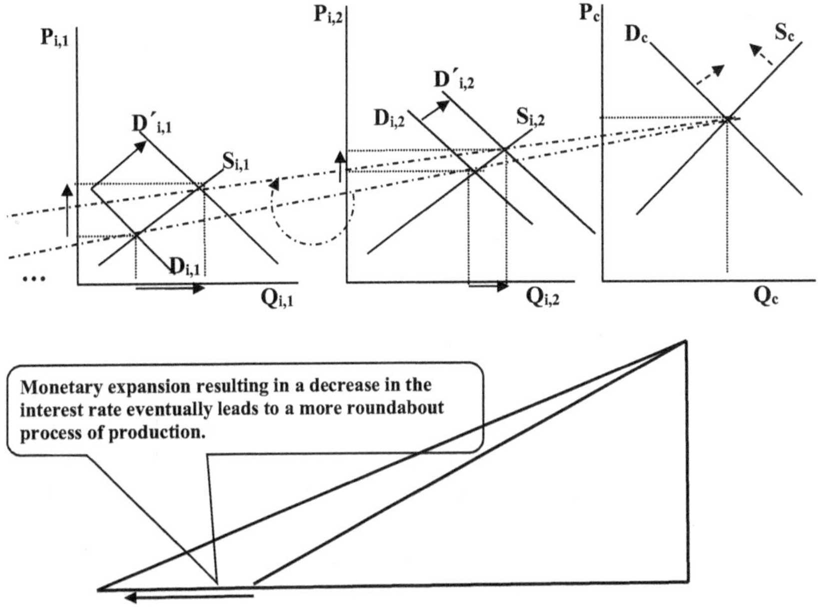

Fig. 5.2 Monetary expansion and the structure of production

in the saving rate. In the graphical model in Fig. 5.2, this fall is thus depicted similarly to the decline in time preference. Growth in demand for production goods raises their prices. They increase relatively more in the stages further from final consumption. In addition, the price ratio between consumption and production goods (P_c/P_i) falls. This fact is reflected in the lower slope of the Hayek triangle, in which the creation of new stages of the production process, very remote from final consumption, can be clearly seen.

One question is crucial in this context: Can higher demand in the early stages be readily met by higher supply? This was the case when time preference declined. However, after the monetary expansion, the market for loanable funds in Fig. 5.1 shows that the flow of real saving decreased rather than increased (to point A). Moreover, the model depicts an excess of investment over (voluntary) saving (distance AB). In contrast to the decline in time preference, consumer demand grows, which is a logical corollary of credit expansion and a falling interest rate.

As a result, the upper right diagram in Fig. 5.2, which represents the consumer goods market, would be more consistent with the market for loanable funds if the demand curve shifted outwards. In turn, this would increase the price of consumption goods. However, even if we consider this option, the slope of the curve connecting the demand curves in the production structure (the dash-dot line) should be flatter due to the decrease in the interest rate.

The direction of the arrows on the quantity axis in Fig. 5.2 shows that they are all inclined to the right, that is, indicating expanding production at each stage of the process, with the strongest rising tendency in the earliest stages. The aforementioned question of whether supply can readily meet demand when all demand curves are increasing does not appear to be answered in the affirmative.

As a first approximation of the whole problem, Hayek ([1931] 1935) assumed that the economy operates at its potential, that is, full-employment level. There are no idle resources that can be mobilized promptly to satisfy increased demand.[2] In such a case, supply can respond only in the stages that have the greatest power to attract the necessary factors of production. Figure 5.2 indicates that these are the stages which are very far from final consumption. Not only do they benefit from a general increase in demand, but another strong impulse in this phase of the production process arises due to the reduced interest rate. Furthermore, it is very likely that, in the real world, a large proportion of new loans are channelled to industrial sectors and other capital-intensive branches of the economy. A key economic reason for this allocation lies in the fact that these sectors are highly sensitive to changes in the interest rate, because they produce capital goods rather than goods very close to final consumption.

This analysis suggests that earlier stages should attract factors of production (mainly labour and other unfinished and capital goods) at the expense of stages close to final consumption. With the acquired factors of production, new capital formation is initiated, and the economy moves on the path of more roundabout processes through capital restructuring, as if time preference has decreased. Nonetheless, in contrast to the decline in time preference, which resulted in lower demand for consumer goods and, consequently, a reduced supply of these goods, the demand for consumption goods after monetary expansion tends to increase. The supply of consumption goods paradoxically falls, as the factors of production have been

[2] The situation of an economy functioning below its potential is discussed in Chap. 8.

moved to earlier stages of production.[3] This relative shortage of consumption goods, which was caused by monetary expansion, is known as "forced saving" (Hayek, 1932). In Fig. 5.2, the forced saving is represented by the distance AB (Horwitz, 2000, p. 113). This type of saving enables the realization of new investment. For some time, it supports the creation of new capital.

The key question is whether this process is sustainable and new capital formation can be completed, that is, whether more roundabout processes will ultimately provide greater output of consumption goods. This does not seem very likely, as the forces of supply and demand at the consumption stage are not mutually consistent. Consumer demand is boosted, but the supply of consumption goods is partly reduced due to the transfer of resources to earlier stages of production. At the same time, the loanable funds model shows that the interest rate is below its natural level.

Austrian business cycle theory predicts that an interest rate gap is not sustainable, and the market interest rate should eventually return to its (initial) natural level. As the interest rate rises, new longer roundabout processes will collapse, because they cannot be completed. The economy will move into a painful recessionary phase, as shown in Fig. 5.3.[4]

It is important to explore the real forces that are in effect when the economy is restructured back to shorter methods. The labour force was first allocated to long production methods, but the reverse process attracts it back to the late stages. The core of this reversion lies in the fact that workers earn newly created money in the form of higher labour incomes. They start to demand more present consumption goods, even though they are engaged in the production of future consumption goods. There is a clear mismatch in the intertemporal structure of demand and supply. Demand for consumption goods is boosted, but the production process has been shaped to supply production goods that will mature into consumption goods in the future. This inconsistency between firm's production plans and consumer demand will drive up not only the prices of consumption goods, but also the price ratio between present and future goods (P_c/P_i). The relative price between consumption goods and production goods increases, which implies that the interest rate must rise.

[3] In Fig. 5.2, the transfer of factors of production from the market of consumption goods could be manifested as an inward shift of the supply curve.

[4] A similar approach arises in Potuzak (2012). Herger (2021) applies the overlapping generations (OLG) model to describe Austrian business cycle theory.

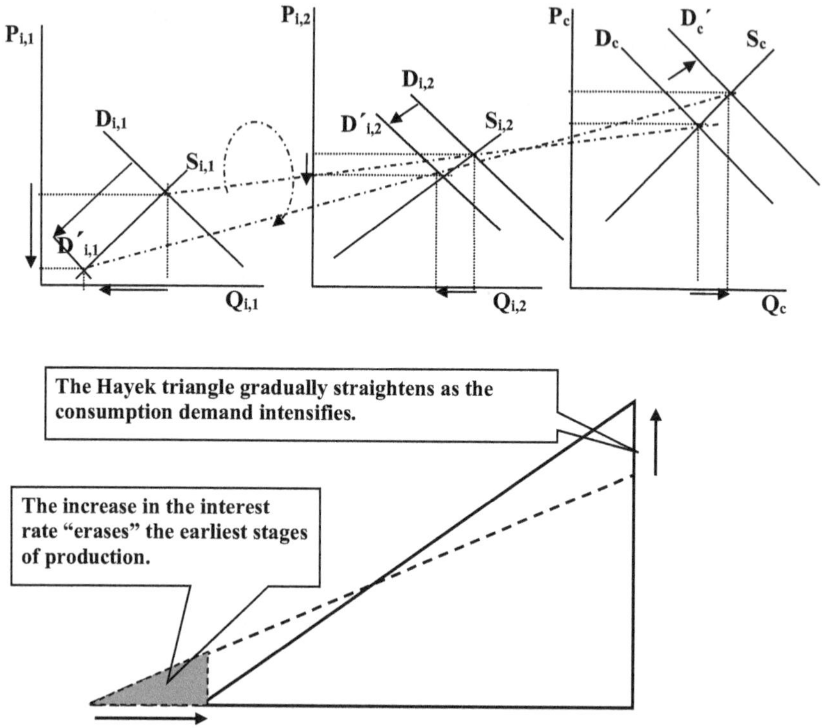

Fig. 5.3 The reversion process of the interest rate and the road to recession

Future consumption goods are produced in the early stages of the production process in the form of capital goods. These processes require the cooperation of the labour force in the future to mature into final consumption goods. This process takes time. However, the labour force (and time) is not available, as it tends to move to stages very close to final consumption, where it is attracted by strong demand for present consumption goods. As a result, there are not enough workers to maintain the production structure, which has been extended due to monetary expansion and artificial interest rate cuts. The labour force is not large enough to meet the high demand for consumption goods and simultaneously to carry out longer methods of the production process. Some roundabout processes must therefore be abandoned, because they cannot compete for labour with late stages. As shown in Fig. 5.3, the structure of the intertemporal demand curves benefits the sectors close to the final consumption stage. The early stages must liquidate their capital and release their labour force into the market.

It is a paradoxical situation. The insufficient amount of labour force required to maintain the expanded capital structure of the economy will lead to unemployment, as sectors that are very remote from the final consumption stage free up labour. Due to the lack of a sufficient labour force to cooperate in the subsequent stages, it is difficult to employ workers in the early stages. The (discounted) value of their marginal product falls sharply due to a drop in demand for the output of capital-creating industries. If the late stages are unable to rapidly absorb the released labour, the economy will experience a period of massive unemployment. Although the economy requires more labour than is available, part of the labour force will be laid off due to a general mismatch between the intertemporal demand and supply.

The time dimension of the entire production process has been extended too far, so there are not enough resources or time to complete all the processes that have been initiated. Scarce resources will be more attracted to the sectors with the highest demand, that is, to the consumption stage and to the stages close to final consumption. Long roundabout processes will be abandoned. In other words, people are too impatient to wait for consumption goods that are produced in the early stages, and which will only mature in the distant future. As a result, the symptom of the crisis is not insufficient consumption, but too much consumption, that is, overconsumption rather than under-consumption (Garrison, 2004). Demand for present consumption goods harms investment and eliminates the creation of new capital structures (Hayek, 1939).

It is not only the labour force that is reduced in the early stages. Figure 5.3 indicates that some capital structures are also abandoned. Because there are not enough resources to complete all the newly launched roundabout processes, part of the capital stock will be lost. This is a paradoxical situation of the simultaneous existence of surplus capital and of a lack of capital (Hayek, 1941). Earlier authors described this as too much circulating capital transformed into fixed capital, so that there is not enough circulating capital to complete fixed capital structures (Wicksell, [1906] 1977). As a result, a large number of unused capital formations are accompanied by insufficient reserves of variable capital. Capital is in both short and excess supply. However, according to Austrian theory, this approach is not general enough. It places too much emphasis on specific forms of capital, and on capital's durability and mobility. The Austrian approach instead stresses the artificial lengthening of production processes and the creation of various capital goods that never mature into final consumption goods due to an insufficient supply of resources and their misallocation (Hayek, 1941, p. 428).

The key reason for the simultaneous existence of too much and too little capital is the mismatch in the intertemporal structure of demand and supply of present and future goods caused by monetary expansion. Monetary forces introduced noise into the price system. The artificially lower interest rate gave a false signal for the allocation of resources, which was not consistent with the planned intertemporal allocation of consumer income. However, it is again the price system that will restore consistency between consumer's consumption plans and firms' production plans. The resulting reallocation will be accompanied by losses of various capital forms, which would not have occurred if economic resources had not been deflected by false price signals coming from the monetary part of the economy.

Figure 5.4 illustrates this dynamic process. It builds upon the tools developed in Fig. 4.6 in Chap. 4. Assume that the economy is in a general intertemporal equilibrium. Between time $t - 5$ and $t - 1$, it provides a steady flow of ten units of consumer goods in each period. The total labour force is five workers, so the final output per worker is two units. In every period, each worker is assigned to a different stage of the production process. For example, in period $t - 4$, one unit of labour creates an intermediate product (capital good) II from intermediate product I, another unit produces capital good I, a third worker completes the whole process, and ten units of consumer goods are supplied to the market.

In each period, the economy employs five units of labour, although some labourers may be voluntarily unemployed because they are looking for a better job. In period $t - 3$, the same processes are repeated as in period $t - 4$. Workers are specialized to take advantage of greater productivity of the division of labour. This results in a given labourer producing the same intermediate product in every period. The worker who created intermediate product II in period $t - 4$ remains in the same occupation and does not move to the production of intermediate III, which is created by another worker in period $t - 3$.

This division of labour is not displayed in Fig. 5.4, although it certainly contributes to the greater productivity of roundabout methods. Five workers can produce ten units of consumption goods in each period if the

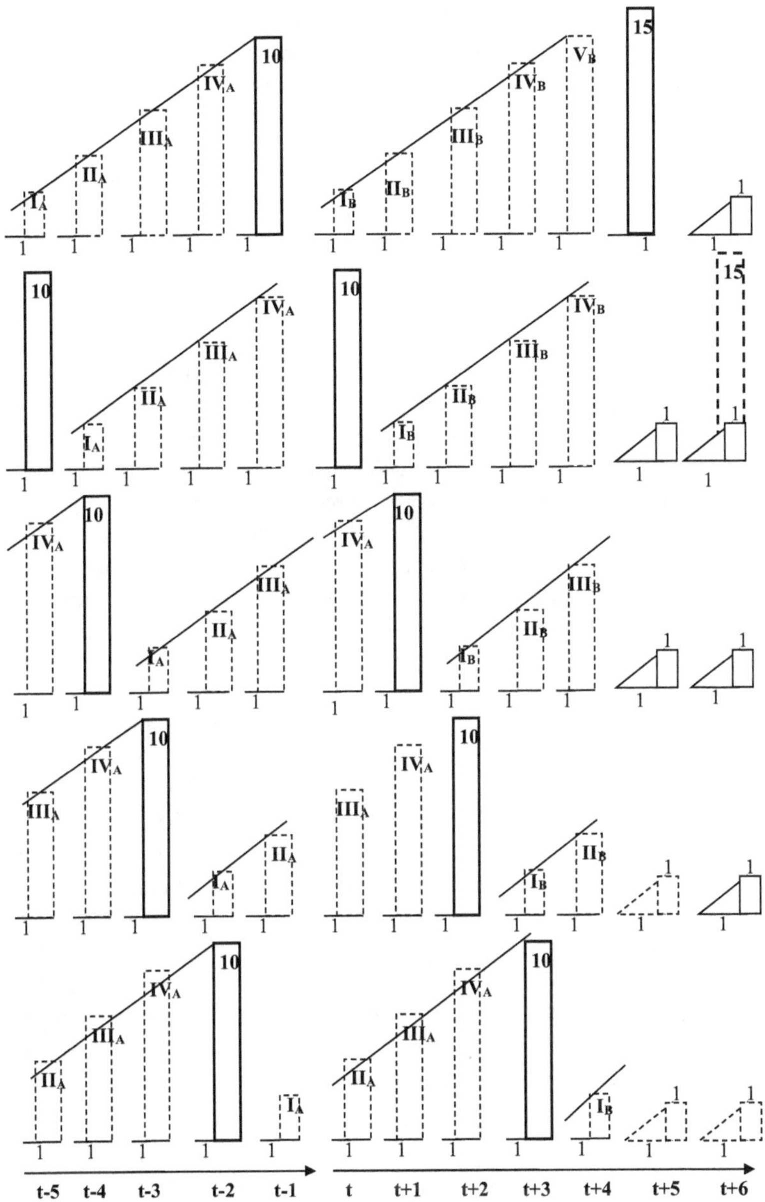

Fig. 5.4 Restructuring of the production processes after monetary expansion

production process is separated and extended to five periods. As discussed in Chap. 2, very short processes that last only one period may create one unit of consumable output per worker, yielding a total output of five units in each period. Longer processes therefore provide twice as many consumer goods as direct methods.

Assume that monetary expansion lowers the interest rate at time *t*, which motivates entrepreneurs to initiate longer production methods. Suppose that in period *t*, the old process, which would supply 10 units of consumption goods in five periods, does not begin, and is replaced by a longer process that provides 15 units in six periods. Roundabout methods are more productive, but take longer and require labour force in the future.

Figure 5.4 assumes that the production structure is transformed only gradually. The second process will be changed to a longer method in period $t + 1$, the third process in period $t + 2$, and so forth.[5] If all these processes are completed, the flow of consumable output can be depicted in panel (a) in Fig. 5.5. It rises from 10 to 15 units. However, every sixth period, the output drops to zero, because only five units of labour are available, while the duration of the longer process is six periods. In addition, at least one worker must be specialized in the production of two types of intermediate products (or an intermediate product and a final consumption good).

In 30 periods, the total output of the longer process can be $(30/6) \times 15 \times 5 = 375$, which yields 75 units of consumption goods per worker in 30 periods, and $75/30 = 2.5$ units per worker in each period. This output is therefore greater than the output of the shorter method, which yields $(30/5) \times 10 \times 5 = 300$ units in 30 periods, 60 units per worker in 30 periods, and 2 units of consumable output per worker in each period.

If monetary expansion and the resulting greater demand can employ labour that was previously unemployed, or if it can speed up the matching process between job seekers and vacancies, the economy can use six units of labour rather than five. The total output of consumption goods over 30 periods will rise to $(30/6) \times 15 \times 6 = 450$. The total output in each period will then increase to $450/30 = 15$ from $375/30 = 12.5$, and there will be no drop in the flow of consumption goods.

[5] The new longer process, which produces 15 units, produces different intermediate products than the relatively shorter process ending in 10 units. We should therefore distinguish between I_A, II_A, III_A, IV_A, and I_B, II_B, III_B, IV_B, V_B in Fig. 5.4. Capital changes not only in terms of size, but also in structure.

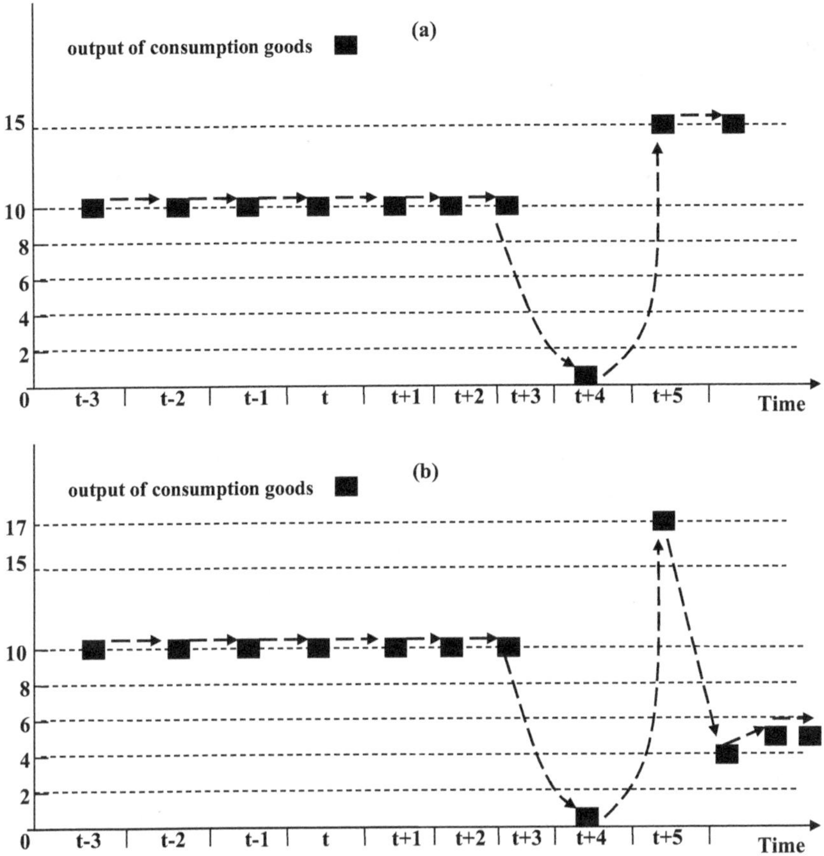

Fig. 5.5 Evolution of the output of consumption goods if the process is not reversed (**a**) and if it is reversed (**b**)

However, according to Austrian theory, production processes lengthened by monetary expansion are not sustainable, because people are too impatient to wait for future output. Figures 5.4 and 5.5 show that consumer goods production drops drastically during period $t + 4$. The process that should provide consumption goods in this particular period has been diverted to a longer method, which will not mature until period $t + 5$.[6]

[6] This observation was also made by Wicksell ([1898] 1936, p. 155), who added that consumers can be partly compensated in the next period when longer methods are completed.

The economy creates an enormous amount of capital goods (intermediate products I_B, II_B, III_B, IV_B, V_B) in period $t + 4$. However, the flow of consumption goods is missing. This drop in consumable output, which will result in a decrease in real consumption, can be regarded as forced saving. In the past, people did not save enough consumer goods to bridge a period of low supply. Monetary expansion diverted the factors of production to longer methods. The output of capital goods is thus at its maximum in period $t + 4$, but people suffer from a shortage of consumption goods in this period.

Suppose that the newly created money is entirely earned by workers in period $t + 4$ and consumption demand is consequently reinforced. The resulting increase in the prices of consumption goods will attract resources to stages that will produce them in a very short time. The longer processes will be abandoned or not resumed. Capital will not be replaced in the early stages, as entrepreneurs are motivated by higher profits to shift factors of production to the late stages to deliver consumer goods as soon as possible.

Assume that all the processes in Fig. 5.4 are drastically shortened to direct methods in period $t + 5$. The only exception is the first long process that provides consumption goods in this particular period. The result is an increase in the output of consumption goods to 17 units in period $t + 5$. Monetary expansion may lead to an extension of the capital structure that will eventually produce fully matured consumption goods. However, this outcome applies only to some processes in the economy, not to all. People are too impatient to allow all lengthened methods to be completed (Hayek, 1935).

In period $t + 5$, a major part of the factors of production are attracted to shorter methods. However, this reallocation takes time, so only some workers can immediately provide consumption goods in direct processes. The output is therefore 17 rather than 19 in period $t + 5$, as shown in Figs. 5.4 and 5.5b. Two units of labour provide neither capital nor consumption goods, because it may be difficult to absorb so much released labour in short processes. Some workers may even be unemployable, owing to a lack of complementary factors of production (Hayek, 1935).

Figure 5.4 indicates that the creation of various capital goods (intermediate products I_B, II_B, III_B, IV_B) between periods $t + 1$ and $t + 4$ was a waste of resources and time. The longer processes in which these capital goods were produced will never be completed. The second process, which would mature into 15 units of consumer goods in period $t + 6$, is an example of this economic loss.

Figure 5.4 also shows that the output of consumption goods drops from 17 to 4 units in period $t + 6$. One worker is still out of the production process. The employed labour force creates a very low output of consumer goods, because the production methods in the economy have been shortened. Along with Hayek (1935), we assume a return to even less roundabout methods than those that prevailed before monetary expansion. The reason is the high demand for present consumption goods, which motivates entrepreneurs to resort to methods that will provide goods very quickly. The evolution of output of consumption goods after monetary expansion is displayed in panel (b) in Fig. 5.5.

There is a significant delay between the moment of monetary expansion and the time when the output of consumption goods is affected. Although the lengthening of the capital structure occurred in our model immediately after the reduction in the interest rate, greater output of consumer goods is delivered later. In addition, the flow of consumption goods is not smooth, as their output eventually declines. The pattern closely resembles a typical sine wave of the business cycle.

There was no indication that the economy was on an unsustainable path. Smooth economic development seems to have been interrupted unexpectedly by a sudden crisis. However, it was monetary expansion that deflected the economy from its long-run intertemporal (dynamic) equilibrium. The business cycle pattern is only a necessary response to this shock, as the economy recedes and then returns to its equilibrium state characterized by consistency between the intertemporal plans of consumers and entrepreneurs.

Because the economy suffers from massive losses of capital structures, labour productivity in the crisis is definitely lower than before. The real wage, defined as the amount of goods an average worker can buy, falls (Hayek, 1942). This effect, together with nominal wage rigidity, may account for the high unemployment rates observed during the recession. Misallocation of resources caused by monetary expansion therefore reduces the well-being of people in the society.

Figure 5.4 shows that the recession's genetic code arises from the boom phase of the cycle. In other words, the current state of the economy is much more important for future performance than might be generally believed. However, the clue cannot be found in a simple autoregressive process of total output or another macroeconomic aggregate. The Austrian explanation of the business cycle is based on the heterogeneity of capital and the consistency of entrepreneur plans at different stages of the production process on the one hand, and intertemporal consumer plans on the other. If this consistency is disrupted, the economic boom will end in recession, even though not one man in a million can recognize that the economy is on an unsustainable path.

The creation of most of the goods that consumers enjoy today began in the past. Similarly, the output of consumption goods in the future depends on the amount of present capital goods and the consistency of production plans among thousands of entrepreneurs. These plans are coordinated both intra-temporally and inter-temporally by the price system. When the price system is disturbed and this coordination is therefore upset, the output of consumption goods is endangered in the future, even if macroeconomic figures indicate that the economy is currently booming.

In Fig. 5.4, monetary expansion as a trigger for the business cycle took place in period t. The time interval between $t + 1$ and $t + 3$ is a period of a seemingly smooth development. Figures 5.4 and 5.5 show that the abundance of capital goods in period $t + 4$ and consumption goods in period $t + 5$ is not sustainable. The economic boom ends in a bust in period $t + 6$. According to Austrian theory, a recession does not arise due to insufficient consumption or investment demand. It is the result of misallocation of resources triggered by monetary expansion. This misallocation manifests itself as an excess of consumption demand at the top of the boom, accompanied by unfinished capital formation, which results in a simultaneous surplus of "fixed" and a shortage of "circulating" capital.

Austrian Business Cycle Theory in the Solow Model

The Solow model was applied in Chap. 4 to clarify some misunderstandings about Austrian capital theory. This model can also be used to add dynamic elements to the loanable funds market. As shown in Fig. 5.1, monetary expansion decreases the market interest rate below the natural level. The quantity of investment rises, while the amount of saving falls. In the Solow model, the discrepancy between these two functions can be depicted as a split of the saving curve sy and the (gross) investment curve $i_G y$. The saving rate thus falls from s_1 to s_2, while the investment rate rises from $i_{G,1}$ to $i_{G,2}$.

The expansion of investment would trigger an accumulation of capital from k_1^* to k_2^* in Fig. 5.6. The reduction in the saving rate would have opposite effects on capital per worker, and the new steady state would be k_3^*. Conflicting forces of investment and saving push the economy to

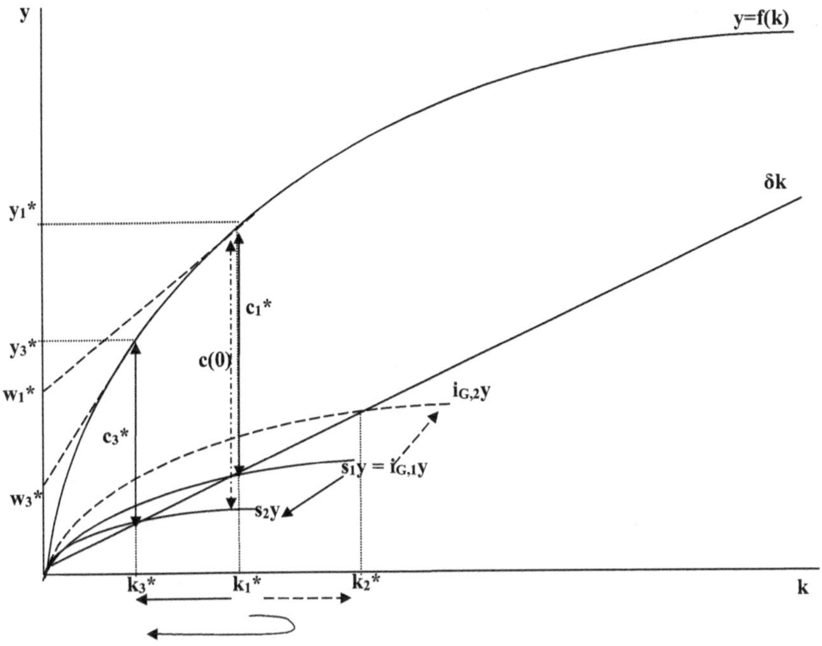

Fig. 5.6 Austrian business cycle theory in the Solow model

different steady states. The diagram also shows that initial consumption rises from c_1^* to $c(0)$ due to a lower saving rate. It is clear that the economy cannot afford more consumption and investment at the same time. This diagram indicates that the economy is moving beyond its production possibilities frontier (Garrison, 2001).

Austrian business cycle theory predicts that the accumulation of capital from k_1^* to k_2^* can only be financed by forced savings, which fills the gap between investment and voluntary saving. However, Austrian theory also states that the given processes of capital accumulation are not sustainable, and economic growth will be reversed. The economy will end up at a lower level of capital per worker k_3^*, with reduced output per worker y_3^*, investment, and consumption per worker c_3^*. Part of the created capital is lost due to misallocation of resources. The Solow model was not designed to depict these disturbances. However, the extension of the model suggested here produces similar predictions as the diagrams in Fig. 5.4, and could be applied to describe some basic dynamics of Austrian business cycle theory.

The new equilibrium in the Solow model k_3^* indicates that monetary expansion and the resulting misallocation of resources not only reduced capital and potential output, but also increased the natural rate of interest, which is equal to $r_3^* = f'(k_3^*) - \delta$. The final real wage w_3^* is lower than the initial w_1^*. The business cycle therefore harms workers. As a result, when we combine neoclassical models with Austrian theory, the business cycle process, although driven by monetary forces, might not leave natural variables at their initial levels. Even in the long run, the monetary sector may not be neutral to the real sector if it delivers false price signals to the markets. [7]

References

Garrison, R. W. (2001). *Time and Money, The Macroeconomics of Capital Structure.* Routledge.

Garrison, R. W. (2004). Overconsumption and Forced Saving in the Mises-Hayek Theory of the Business Cycle. *History of Political Economy, 36*(2), 323–349.

von Hayek, F. A. (1932). A Note on the Development of the Doctrine of 'Forced Saving'. *The Quarterly Journal of Economics, 47*(1), 123–133.

von Hayek, F. A. (1935 [1931]). *Prices and Production* (2nd ed.). Augustus M. Kelly.

von Hayek, F. A. (1939). *Profits, Interest and Investment.* George Routledge & Sons Ltd.

von Hayek, F. A. (1941). *The Pure Theory of Capital.* The University of Chicago Press.

von Hayek, F. A. (1942). The Ricardo Effect. *Economica, 9*(34), 127–152.

Herger, N. (2021). Mr. Hayek and the Classics: A Suggested Interpretation of the Business Cycle Theory in Prices and Production. *The Quarterly Journal of Austrian Economics, 24*(1), 79–109.

Horwitz, S. (2000). *Microfoundations and Macroeconomics: An Austrian Perspective.* Routledge.

von Mises, L. (2009 [1912]). *Theory of Money and Credit.* Ludwig von Mises Institute.

O'Driscoll, G. P., Jr., & Rizzo, M. J. (1996). *The Economics of Time and Ignorance* (2nd ed.). Routledge.

[7] Salter and Luther (2016) apply a three-dimensional model to describe a path of the economy to lower production possibilities frontier (PPF), extending the approach of Garrison (2001).

Potuzak, P. (2012). Some Elucidations in the Austrian Business Cycle Theory. *Journal of International Scientific Publications, 6*(3), 96–132.
Salter, A. W., & Luther, W. J. (2016). The Optimal Austrian Business Cycle Theory. In S. Horwitz (Ed.), *Studies in Austrian Macroeconomics, Advances in Austrian Economics, Volume 20*. Emerald Group Publishing Limited.
Wicksell, K. (1936 [1898]). *Interest and Prices*. Augustus M. Kelley.
Wicksell, K. (1977 [1906]). *Lectures on Political Economy, Volume 2*. Augustus M. Kelley.

CHAPTER 6

The Dynamics of the Interest Rate in Austrian Business Cycle Theory

Monetary expansion lowers the interest rate below the natural level. Endogenous economic forces tend to push it back. This chapter focuses on this return of the market interest rate to its natural level during the business cycle. The explanation for this dynamics is not uniform in the Austrian school. However, it is essential to explain economic fluctuations. This section compares the main contributions of Friedrich August von Hayek, Ludwig von Mises, and Murray N. Rothbard to this issue, and emphasizes some inconsistencies that emerged in the analysis of this phenomenon.

Hayek (1935) considered the interest rate primarily as a price margin between two successive stages of production. The lower the price margin, the longer production methods the economy can afford. Monetary expansion decreases price margins and allows the production structure to be lengthened. This leads to more capital-intensive methods of production. The new structure can be built by labour (and other factors of production) previously employed in the late production stages by offering workers higher wages. Through this channel, the newly created money is obtained by the owners of various factors of production. Workers, now in the role of consumers, are highly unlikely to dramatically change the time shape of their income in favour of more distant future consumption goods, whose production has been initiated in the form of production goods.[1]

[1] This part of the Hayek's theory was criticized by Sraffa (1932).

P. Potuzak, *Austrian Theory of Capital and Business Cycle*, https://doi.org/10.1007/978-3-031-18728-5_6

In fact, the opposite can be expected, because the interest rate has fallen. Increased demand from workers for present consumer goods will lead to significant upward pressure on the prices of these goods, supported by the outflow of resources to earlier stages of production. The rise in the price of consumption goods will eventually result in an increase in price margins (P_c/P_i), back to the level where this ratio was before the monetary expansion.

This explanation is at the heart of the Hayekian approach to the interest-rate reversion process. The Hayek triangle changes its slope, and the earlier stages of production are abandoned as the higher interest rate decreases the demand for their output. Figure 5.3 in Chap. 5 shows that the fall in prices is particularly strong in the earliest stages of production, that is, in the stages that experienced the greatest price increase after monetary expansion.

As Hayek put it:

At the same time incomes of wage earners will be rising in consequence of the increased amount of money available for investment by entrepreneurs. There can be little doubt that in the face of rising prices of consumers' goods these increases will be spent on such goods and so contribute to drive up their prices even faster. These decisions will not change the amount of consumers' goods immediately available, though it may change their distribution between individuals. But—and this is the fundamental point—it will mean a new and reversed change of the proportion between the demand for consumers' goods and the demand for producers' goods in favour of the former. The prices of consumers' goods will therefore rise relatively to the prices of producers' goods. And this rise of the prices of consumers' goods will be the more marked because it is the consequence not only of an increased demand for consumers' goods but an increase in the demand as measured in money. All this must mean a return to shorter or less roundabout methods of production if the increase in the demand for consumers' goods is not compensated by a further proportional injection of money by new bank loans granted to producers.

Hayek (1935, p. 89)

This point of view is perfectly consistent with Hayek's earlier approach:

If, however, the fall in the rate of interest is due to an increase in the circulating media, it can never lead to a corresponding diminution in the price margin, or to a readjustment of the two sets of prices to the level of an equilibrium rate of interest which will endure. In this case, moreover, the increased demand for investment goods will bring about a net increase in the demand for consumption goods; and therefore the price margin cannot be narrowed more than is permitted by the time-lag in the rise of consumption goods prices—a lag existing only as long as the process of inflation continues. As soon as the cessation of credit inflation puts a stop to the rise in the prices of investment goods, the difference between these and the prices of consumption goods will increase again, not only to its previous level but beyond, since, in the course of inflation, the structure of production has been so shifted that in comparison with the division of the social income between expenditure and saving the supply of consumption goods will be relatively less, and that of production goods relatively greater, than before the inflation began.

Hayek ([1929] 1933, p. 217)

The price ratio of consumption goods to producer goods plays the key role in Hayek's explanation. It determines the maximum length of the production process the economy can afford. For Hayek, the general price level is by no means as important as the structure of relative prices, which makes his approach significantly different from modern business cycle theories.

Hayek (1935) acknowledged the important contribution of his predecessor, Ludwig von Mises, but also criticized him for emphasizing changes in the purchasing power of money rather than relative prices when examining the business cycle. Mises is considered to have been the founder of the Austrian business cycle theory. His approach resembles a more elaborate Hayek's theory. In his first opus, Mises ([1912] 2009) analysed the effects of changes in the quantity of money on the interest rate. According to Mises, money expansion first lowers the interest rate and triggers more roundabout methods of production. Sooner or later, however, the so-called subsistence fund[2] is exhausted, resulting in a lack of consumption goods and an increase in their prices. This, in turn, leads to a rise in the interest rate, because the price difference between consumption goods and production goods widens. Mises suggested that the increase in the interest rate is further reinforced by the decline in the objective purchasing power of money.

The following passages document his approach:

The increased productive activity that sets in when the banks start the policy of granting loans at less than the natural rate of interest at first causes the prices

[2] The subsistence fund theory is criticized in Hayek (1935, 1941).

> *of production goods to rise while the prices of consumption goods, although they rise also, do so only in a moderate degree, viz., only in so far as they are raised by the rise in wages. Thus the tendency towards a fall in the rate of interest on loans that originates in the policy of the banks is at first strengthened. But soon a counter-movement sets in: the prices of consumption goods rise, those of production goods fall. That is, the rate of interest on loans rises again, it again approaches the natural rate.*
>
> Mises ([1912] 2009, pp. 362-363)

> *This counter-movement is now strengthened by the fact that the increase of the stock of money in the broader sense that is involved in the increase in the quantity of fiduciary media reduces the objective exchange-value of money. Now, as has been shown, so long as this depreciation of money is going on, the rate of interest on loans must rise above the level that would be demanded and paid if the objective exchange-value of money remained unaltered.*
>
> Mises ([1912] 2009, p. 363)

In his later work, Mises ([1949] 1996) relied heavily on changes in the purchasing power of money to analyse interest rate dynamics over the business cycle. His reasoning is similar to that of Fisher (1930), as he assumed that an expected decline in the purchasing power of money would lead to an increase in the interest rate. Mises called the interest rate component that responds to changes in the purchasing power of money a price premium.

Mises (1996) argued that the magnitude of the initial interest rate cut is closely related to the relative amount of money injected into the credit markets compared to the quantity flowing into the consumer goods markets. According to Mises, if money growth were directed only at consumer markets, interest rates would not decline.[3] If the interest rate is reduced, the business cycle is triggered. The rise in the quantity of money will eventually depress the general purchasing power of money (i.e. increase the price level). This widespread increase in prices will be manifested in higher interest rates due to the price premium. Finally, a higher interest rate should disrupt the process initiated by monetary expansion, and the economy is on the path to recession.

However, the key problem is whether the price premium can raise both the nominal interest rate and the real interest rate, or whether the real interest rate remains artificially low, below its natural level. For the real

[3] A similar statement can be found in Hayek (1935) and Garrison (2001).

interest rate to return to its natural level, the increase in the nominal interest rate must be higher than the rise in the rate of inflation. It is therefore not sufficient to explain that the interest rate increases due to the fall in the purchasing power of money. If the nominal interest rate does not keep pace with inflation, the real interest rate may remain below its natural level, which will result in further lengthening of the production structure. Mises (1996) himself mentioned this problem. This is discussed in more detail in the section investigating "The Dynamics of the Money Supply".

Thus, the explanation for interest rate reversion cannot hinge only on the general increase in prices. A more important component is the movement of Hayek's price margins, expressed roughly as the ratio between the prices of consumer goods and production goods (P_c/P_i). The real interest rate, which is a specific relative price, is reflected in the (logarithmic) price difference between the goods at different stages of processing, regardless of the evolution of the general price level. Although this ratio declines after the expansion of the money supply, it will eventually increase due to growing demand for consumption goods when newly created money is earned by workers in the form of higher wages. In this phase of the business cycle, prices of consumption goods rise faster than prices of capital goods because factors of production were attracted to the production of producer goods at the expense of consumption goods. It is the relative scarcity of present consumption goods compared to production goods, which represent future consumption goods that are currently in various stages of processing, that will cause the real interest rate to return to its previous level.

The entire process is illustrated in Fig. 6.1. Firstly, the monetary expansion reduces the real interest rate (P_c/P_i ratio) from 4% (102/98) to 2% (102/100). However, economic forces clarified in the analysis push the real interest rate back to 4% (104/100). Monetary expansion can also raise the general price level, for example by 10%, which will increase the nominal interest rate to 14%. Because the production process takes place over time, the nominal interest rate is calculated by comparing the initial value of unfinished goods at time t_0 (i.e. 100) with the value of more processed goods at time t_1 (i.e. 114).[4]

Rothbard (2004), another important proponent of Austrian business cycle theory, built upon the findings of Mises and Hayek. Several new

[4] A discussion of the correct calculation of the interest rate in a time-consuming process of production appears in Rothbard (2004).

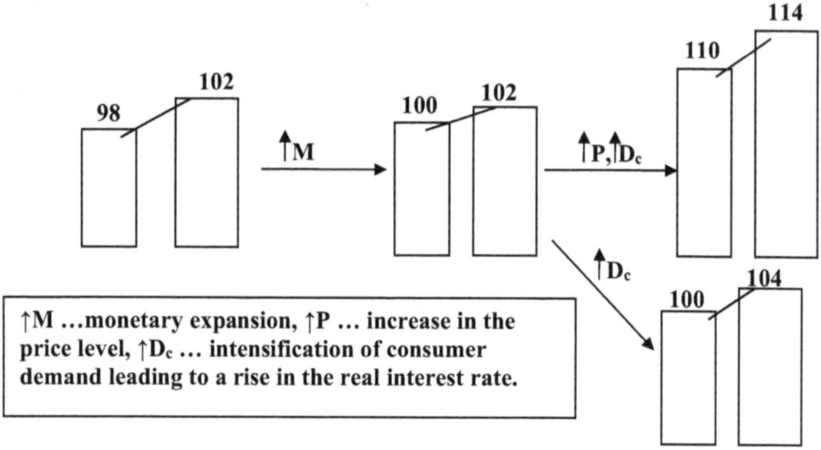

Fig. 6.1 The dynamics of the interest rate in the Misesian system

ideas are included in his explanation. Rothbard's approach to interest rate dynamics is as follows:

> *The owners of the original factors, with their increased money income, naturally hasten to spend their new money. They allocate this spending between consumption and investment in accordance with their time preferences. Let us assume that the time-preference schedules of the people remain unchanged. This is a proper assumption, since there is no reason to assume that they have changed because of the inflation. Production now no longer reflects voluntary time preferences. Business has been led by credit expansion to invest in higher stages, as if more savings were available. Since they are not, business has overinvested in the higher stages and underinvested in the lower. Consumers act promptly to re-establish their time preferences—their preferred investment/consumption proportions and price differentials. The differentials will be re-established at the old, higher amount, i.e., the rate of interest will return to its free-market magnitude. As a result, the prices at the higher stages of production will fall drastically, the prices at the lower stages will rise again, and the entire new investment at the higher stages will have to be abandoned or sacrificed.*
> Rothbard ([1962] 2004, p. 996)

Rothbard (2004) mentioned one important idea that was also discussed by Hayek (1935) and Mises (2009). It was demonstrated that the (real) interest rate will eventually return to its previous natural level. This assumption de facto implies that money is neutral in the long run because it does not affect the natural interest rate, which could be accepted as a first approximation of reality. However, the Austrian authors extend their analysis using the following findings: The injection of money into the economy will never enter all markets at the same time or with the same intensity, so the prices of various goods will not be affected equally. Even in the long run, the resulting structures of relative prices may be different than they were in the period before expansion. The money stream injected into the economy changes the incomes and wealth of people unevenly, because the effects depend on an individual's proximity to the new inflow of money. Some people gain, while others may lose. Because people differ in their time preferences, the aggregate saving curve will end up in a different position than it was before monetary expansion.

It would be quite surprising if the second blade of the Marshallian scissors on the loanable funds market, that is, investment, did not change its position as well. According to Austrian business cycle theory, economy-wide fluctuations cause large-scale capital losses. As a result, the final position of the curve of the marginal product of capital is unknown. Since monetary disturbances and the resulting business cycle will affect both curves in the loanable funds market, it is not possible to determine the eventual level of the natural rate of interest.

> *A precise re-establishment of the old price-ratios between production goods and consumption goods is not possible, on the one hand because the intervention of the banks has brought about a re-distribution of property, and on the other hand because the automatic recovery of the loan market involves certain of the phenomena of a crisis, which are signs of the loss of some of the capital invested in the excessively-lengthened roundabout processes of production.*
> Mises ([1912] 2009, p. 364)

In the Austrian model, money is not neutral, even in the long run.[5] However, this long-run non-neutrality of money differs substantially from

[5] The non-neutrality of money in the Austrian model is emphasized by Coyne and Boettke (2020, p. 44). Horwitz (2016) elucidates Hayek's approach to neutral money in detail. Potuzak (2016, 2017, 2018) analyses Hayek's proposal to minimize the real effects of money on the economy by stabilizing MV, rather than by stabilizing the price level P, in the equation of exchange $MV = PY$. White (1999) discusses the possible contradictions of Hayek's proposals for stabilizing the money stream MV or the price level P, which Hayek formulated at different times in his career.

the well-known New Keynesian theory of hysteresis. The New Keynesian theory developed an idea that monetary restriction or expansion can affect the natural rate of unemployment. A loose monetary policy may decrease the natural unemployment rate, because it is attracted to the lower actual unemployment rate, whereas a tighter monetary policy may leave scars on the economy in the form of a persistently higher unemployment rate (Mankiw & Romer, 1991a, 1991b).

By no means does Austrian theory suggest that monetary expansion could permanently reduce both the market and the natural rate of interest, thereby supporting faster economic growth with lower unemployment, as some New Keynesians might argue. As shown earlier, monetary expansion may disturb the equilibrium, so the final level of the natural interest rate is not determined. At the same time, monetary expansion temporarily deflects the interest rate from its natural level and triggers the business cycle rather than sustainable economic growth. This results in a loss of capital rather than creation of new capital, and is therefore highly unlikely to reduce the natural unemployment rate. In fact, it is reasonable to expect the opposite movement.

The evolution of the interest rate in Austrian business cycle theory is depicted in Fig. 6.2. The diagram shows that at time t_0, monetary expansion decreases both the nominal (i) and real (r) rates of interest below the natural level. At one point in the future, the process will reverse. It is reasonable to expect the nominal interest rate to start rising earlier than the real interest rate ($t_1 < t_2$), because its growth is driven by yet another source: price inflation.[6]

The eventual level of both rates cannot be predicted. The nominal interest rate will presumably exceed its initial level, because it is influenced by a higher inflation rate. The primary reason for the final indeterminacy of the market interest rate (solid line) is the unknown path of the natural rate of interest (dashed line) after monetary expansion. In Austrian theory, the market interest rate is attracted to the natural level, although the deviation of the market interest rate from its natural level caused by a monetary shock can lead to a change in the natural interest rate itself.

[6] As Fig. 6.2 shows, there is a period (from t_1 to t_2) in which the nominal interest rate rises, but the real rate continues to decline. This lag of the real interest rate behind the nominal rate was mentioned by Fisher (1930), who wrote that the nominal interest rate may not respond sufficiently (in terms of time or level) to inflation, which leads to a fall in the real interest rate.

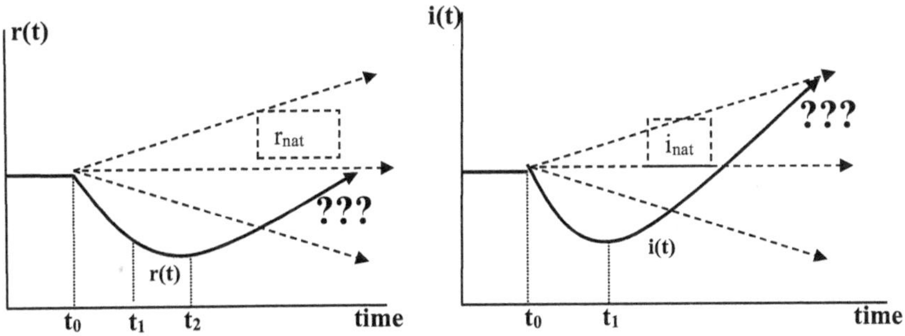

Fig. 6.2 The indeterminacy of the eventual level of the interest rates

Hayek Strikes Back: The Ricardo Effect

In the late 1930s and early 1940s, Hayek refined his theory and introduced a novel argument to support his previous findings. However, this new approach was soon subjected to sharp criticism, which led to the eventual victory of the Keynesian Revolution.[7]

Hayek's analysis begins at the top of the boom phase of the business cycle, in which consumer demand is reinforced by higher earnings of primary factors of production (especially labour). Markets for consumption goods experience a positive demand shock, which leads to higher prices. At this stage of the process, Hayek assumed that consumer price inflation outpaced wage growth. Thus, real wages, which Hayek defined as the ratio between nominal wages and the price of goods produced by the given labour, fall. Consistent with this analysis, Hayek argued that price margins (which he called profit margins in his later works) rise. In this phase of the business cycle, Hayek proved that this particular movement in profit margins inevitably leads to a shortening of production techniques and the substitution of labour for capital. Entrepreneurs abandon the most roundabout methods initiated at the beginning of the boom. Hayek's new argument was designed to offer additional reasons for straightening the Hayek triangle at the end of the boom and the outset of the recession.

Hayek (1942a) again argued that an increase in consumer demand at the top of the boom would lead to a reduction in investment spending. However, he added one important assumption. Entrepreneurs cannot borrow money on credit markets. Hayek therefore analysed a situation in

[7] A new approach appears in Hayek (1939, 1941, 1942a), a critique of it is in Kaldor (1942), and Hayek's subsequent reaction is in Hayek (1942b).

which profit margins grow, while access to new loans is limited. This assumption bypassed the influence of the loanable funds market and focused solely on processes within one firm.

The key question is what production techniques entrepreneurs should apply when profit margins increase. Consider Hayek's (1942a) own numerical example, extended by further calculations. Imagine a hypothetical firm that has three different methods of producing a given output. In the beginning, all three techniques earn the same profit rate. The firm is therefore indifferent as to which is used.

The first method is characterized by a very low profit margin, say 1% (e.g. an entrepreneur buys inputs for 100 and sells output for 101), but the rate of turnover of this method is relatively high. The firm can repeat this production process six times per year, from the purchase of inputs to the sale of the final output, because the final output matures in just two months. As a result, the profit rate on an annual basis is about 6% (exactly 6.15%).

The second method turns over the firm's capital once a year, and also has a 6% profit rate. For example, it buys inputs for 95 at the beginning of the year, and sells the output for 101 at the end of the year. Finally, the profit margin of the third method is high (80%), but the turnover is very long. The firm buys inputs for 56 and sells the output 10 years later for 101. The annual profit rate of this highly roundabout production method is also 6%.

As assumed earlier, the economy is at the top of the boom and production techniques have been lengthened due to artificial interest rate cuts. The newly created money is earned by workers who try to restore their real consumption, which was reduced due to shifting of resources to earlier stages of production.[8] At this point, strong demand flows into the consumption goods markets, which leads to an increase in their prices by, say, 5% (from 101 to 106). This rise in the prices of consumption goods cannot leave the profit margins and profit rates of the various production methods unaltered.

The profit margin of the first method rises from 1% to 6% (106/100), but the annual profit rate skyrockets from 6% to 42% (without compounding to 36% = 6 × 6%). The second method records an increase to 11% (106/95), and the third, most roundabout, technique will be almost unaffected. The annual profit rate will rise by only 0.6 p.p. to 6.6%.[9]

[8] This is exactly the moment when forced saving ends, because the workers have finally received the newly created money.

[9] $(106/56)^{1/10}-1 = 0.066 = 6.6\%$.

Such abrupt changes in the relative profitability of various production methods should induce entrepreneurs to use techniques that achieve final output as quickly as possible. Firms will be motivated to reduce the length of production processes. Hayek (1942a) proposed various ways to speed up the production process. Firms may substitute labour-intensive methods for labour-saving methods. They can overuse the capital goods at their disposal or terminate investment in depreciated capital units.

This effect, which Hayek termed the Ricardo effect, supports the fundamental conclusion of the Austrian theory that the rise in consumer demand will lead to a reduction in the length of the production process. This can be demonstrated by shortening the Hayek triangle. The main reason is that an increase in the profit rate favours production techniques that generate consumer goods in a shorter time period.

One important objection was raised by Kaldor (1942), which is the basis of the next section. From Kaldor's point of view, it is absurd to assume that an increase in the rate of profit should reduce, rather than expand, the invested capital. After all, it is the growth of profitability (the marginal product of capital) that leads to an increase in investment spending. One possible solution to this criticism is proposed in the following section.

Confusion in Austrian Business Cycle Theory

In this section, we clarify some ambiguities, misunderstandings, and contradictions that can be detected in the Austrian analysis. At first glance, they might seem trivial. However, because the original authors did not use much graphical or even mathematical apparatus, they provoked discussion among both adherents and critics of Austrian theory.

The dynamics of the interest rate in Austrian business cycle theory can be portrayed by the following chain of implications:

1. Monetary expansion lowers interest rates, which motivates entrepreneurs to increase investment spending.
2. However, massive investment demand should eventually raise interest rates.
3. Ultimately, higher interest rates depress capital expenditures and trigger a recession.

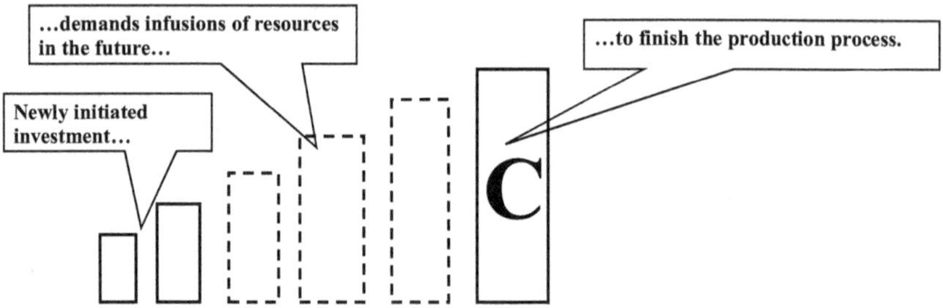

Fig. 6.3 Investment that demands further investment

There is no need for any in-depth scientific research to clarify that the aforementioned statement is a clear example of circular reasoning. In particular, the implications do not distinguish between moving along the (investment) curve and shifting the entire curve. The first confusion is in the second sentence, but the most serious problem is in the logical connections between the sentences. The following paragraphs explain the sources of this confusion.

It is clear from Fig. 5.1 in Chap. 5 that monetary expansion lowers the market interest rate. This interest rate cut results in a growth in investment. However, a more accurate conclusion should be that the decline in the interest rate increases the quantity of investment. There is no shift of the entire investment curve. Therefore, there can be no consequent increase in the interest rate, as suggested in the second aforementioned statement. In other words, the second statement is by no means implied by the first statement.

The fundamental problem rests in the fact that Austrian theory is a dynamic theory, while the neoclassical loanable funds market is a static model. Hayek (1937) identified one important fact in this respect. The investment initiated today will require additional capital investment in the future if the entire process of capital formation is to be completed. This idea is depicted in Fig. 6.3.

Other important Hayek's insights are in the following paragraphs:

> *Anything which will lead people to expect a lower rate of interest, or a larger supply of investible funds, than will actually exist when the time comes for their utilization, will in the way we have suggested force interest rates to rise much higher than would have been the case if people had not expected such a low rate.*
> Hayek (1937, p. 176)

An increase in the rate of investment, or the quantity of capital goods, may have the effect of raising rather than lowering the rate of interest, if this increase has given rise to expectation of greater future supply of investible funds than is actually forthcoming.

Hayek (1937, p. 176)

Hayek's words suggest that the interest rate tends to rise when the expected flow of saving (or rather the supply of loanable funds, which may also be driven by monetary expansion) does not materialize. The unjustified increase in investment, which will eventually lack the necessary savings, will trigger a sharp rise in the interest rate when this error is identified. We return to this phenomenon later.

The second and more important problem in sound reasoning is the implication between statements 2 and 3. As mentioned, Kaldor (1942) subjected Hayek's theory to criticism. [10] If the profitability of firms grows at the end of the boom, this should undoubtedly result in a shift of the investment curve outwards. Figure 6.4 shows that this movement of the investment curve will increase the market interest rate.[11] However, the total quantity of capital invested can never decline, as suggested by statement 3, unless the saving curve has a perverse downward-sloping shape.[12]

[10] The dispute between Hayek and Kaldor is discussed in more detail in Moss and Vaughn (2010) and Klausinger (2011). The Ricardo effect is critically analysed by Zijp (1992, 56ff.) and Cowen (1997, p. 107).

[11] O'Driscoll and Rizzo (1996, p. 209) also indicate the outward shift of the investment curve.

[12] Some traces of similar confusion can also be found in Mises (1996, p. 553):

Of course, in order to continue production on the enlarged scale brought about by the expansion of credit, all entrepreneurs, those who did expand their activities no less than those who produce only within the limits in which they produced previously, need additional funds as the costs of production are now higher. If the credit expansion consists merely in a single, not repeated injection of a definite amount of fiduciary media into the loan market and then ceases altogether, the boom must very soon stop. The entrepreneurs cannot procure the funds they need for the further conduct of their ventures. This gross market rate of interest rises because the increased demand for loans is not counterpoised by a corresponding increase in the quantity of money available for lending.

And in Garrison (2001, p. 72):

The bidding for increasingly scarce resources and the accompanying increased demands for credit put upward pressure on the interest rate.

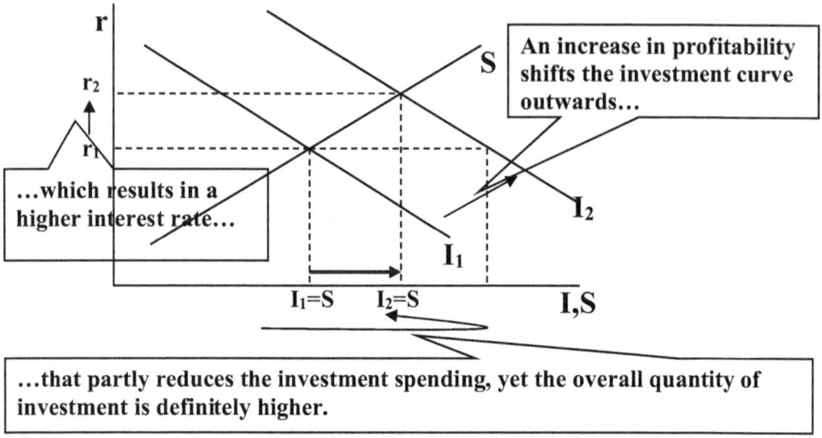

Fig. 6.4 Ricardo effect in Kaldor's reasoning

Assuming a standard shape of the saving curve, the volume of saving should increase, which will finance higher investment. According to Kaldor, higher profitability can never induce the liquidation of capital and a consequent recession, as Hayek consistently asserted. In graphical terms, it is unlikely that higher profit margins could ever straighten the Hayek triangle and erase the earliest stages of production, illustrated by the grey area in Fig. 5.3 in Chap. 5.

At first glance, Austrian theory does not seem to stand up to Kaldor's critique. However, Kaldor omitted one important step in the Austrian reasoning. It is undoubtedly true that rising consumer prices lead to higher profitability. However, this price increase is caused by reinforced consumer demand, as explained in previous sections. This resurrection of demand for present consumption goods represents the end of forced saving. In other words, higher consumption reduces saving in the economy. This must result in an increase in the interest rate. Consistently with the rising interest rate, profit margins (P_c/P_i) grow, as do the prices of consumer goods. Figure 6.5 illustrates the decline in saving represented by the inward shift of the saving curve, which raises the market interest rate.

As Fig. 6.5 shows, the increase in the interest rate reduces, rather than raises, the amount of investment. The rise in the interest rate results in a shortening of the Hayek triangle and a reduction of the length of production methods. Figure 6.6 illustrates this abrupt shortening, which is

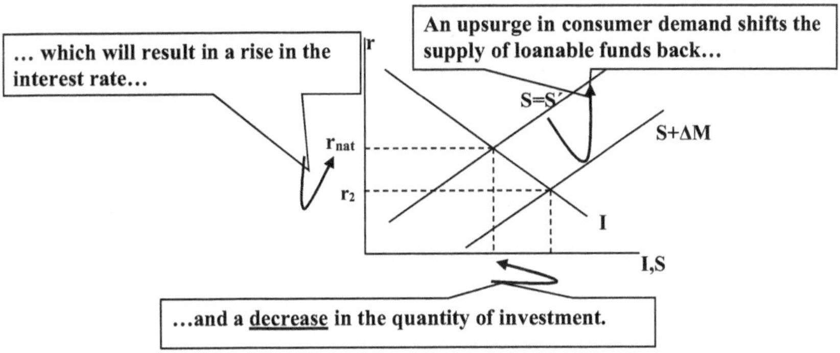

Fig. 6.5 The reversion of the interest rate in Austrian theory

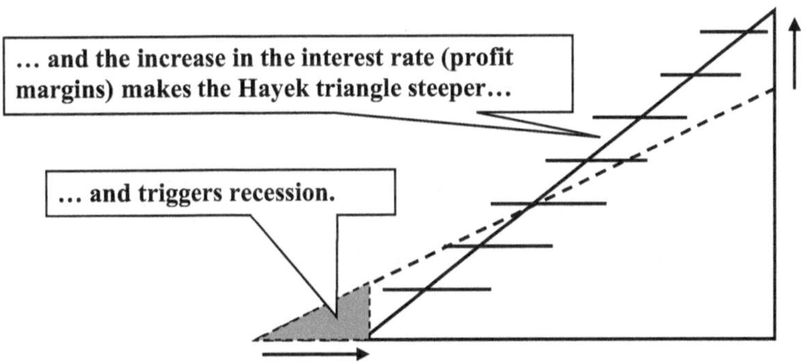

Fig. 6.6 Straightening the Hayek triangle: a road to recession

accompanied by massive losses of the artificially created capital, especially in the early stages of the production process. This can be identified as a recession. In addition, the marginal product of capital rises, as the upward movement along the investment curve in Fig. 6.5 shows. Profit margins grow, which completes the logical chain of Austrian reasoning.

Analysis shows that high profit margins are consistent with reductions of capital stock. At the top of the boom, Austrian theory predicts a relative decline in savings (i.e. an inward shift of the saving curve, which reduces the quantity of investment), rather than an outward shift of the investment curve, which may result in a greater quantity of saving. The interest rate rises in the market for loanable funds due to lower supply, not higher

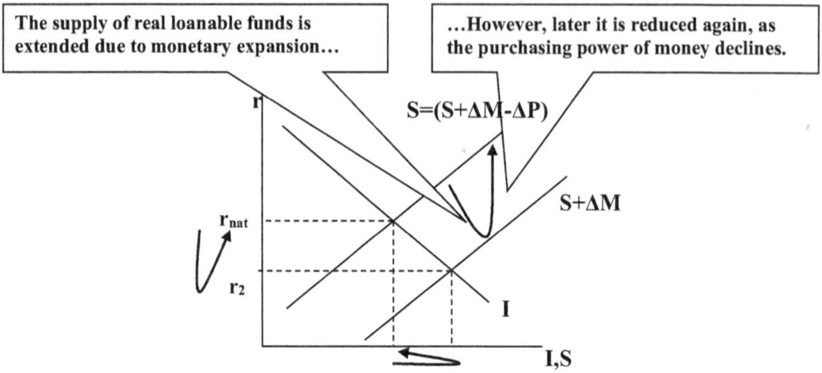

Fig. 6.7 Reversion of the interest rate based on the decline in the purchasing power of money

demand. The key remaining question is what phenomenon shifts the saving curve inwards, because only this movement protects Austrian theory from Kaldor's criticism.

The first solution lies in Mises's theory. In the previous analysis, the market for loanable funds has been assumed to be a model with real saving, real investment, and a real interest rate. However, because the intermediation between saving and investment takes place in the real world in the form of money, the initial increase in the supply of credit, caused by pure monetary expansion on the part of the banking sector, undoubtedly leads to an extension of the supply of real loanable funds.[13] The presence of a higher real supply in the credit market cuts the real interest rate, which acts as a signal to entrepreneurs that more real resources can be used to create new capital. Sooner or later, as Mises argued, monetary expansion will be reflected in lower purchasing power of money, which will reduce the supply of real loanable funds to the previous level. The main reason for this is that a higher price level decreases the purchasing power of funds raised by entrepreneurs and diminishes the real amount of resources that they can attract. This type of reversion process is illustrated in Fig. 6.7.

[13] At this point, it would be better to avoid the term "expansion of real savings". The injection of money into the system extends the supply of real funds available to firms. Using the term "increase in real savings" would suggest that monetary expansion leads to higher saving by people, which is of course not the case; rather, the opposite is true.

However, the question is whether this movement of the curve representing the supply of real loanable funds is justifiable. As analysed earlier, the rising price level may only increase the nominal interest rate, while the real rate remains unchanged. It is therefore possible that monetary expansion would permanently depress the real interest rate. As a result, the crucial reversion dynamics of the interest rate will never occur. Figure 6.8 demonstrates this process, where variables are expressed in nominal rather than real terms.

Figure 6.8 shows that monetary expansion depresses the nominal interest rate from i_1 to i_2. The gradually increasing price level resulting from monetary expansion will raise expectations on the part of both savers and entrepreneurs. Savers will save less in anticipation that money will have lower purchasing power in the future. The saving curve moves to the left from $(S + \Delta M)$ to S'. In contrast, entrepreneurs are ready to invest more at a given nominal interest rate, with debts repaid in the future in depreciated money. The investment function shifts outwards from I to I′. Both movements push the nominal interest rate up to i_3. This process, known as the Fisher effect, increases the nominal interest rate one-to-one with inflation, but the real interest rate may remain artificially lower. The problem is that there may not be any mechanism to compensate for the initial decrease in the interest rate caused by the expansion of the money supply. With the real interest rate permanently depressed, investment can be continually supported.

The solution to this apparent puzzle can be found in mainstream New Keynesian/monetarist theory. The previous analysis does not fully explore the time horizon of the entire process and the dynamics of the money

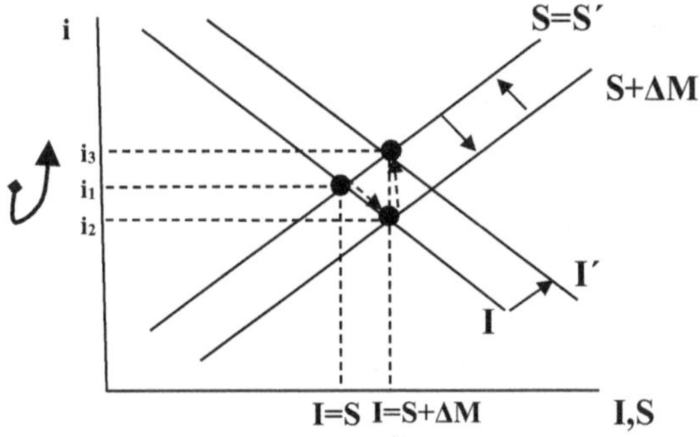

Fig. 6.8 Monetary expansion and the Fisher effect

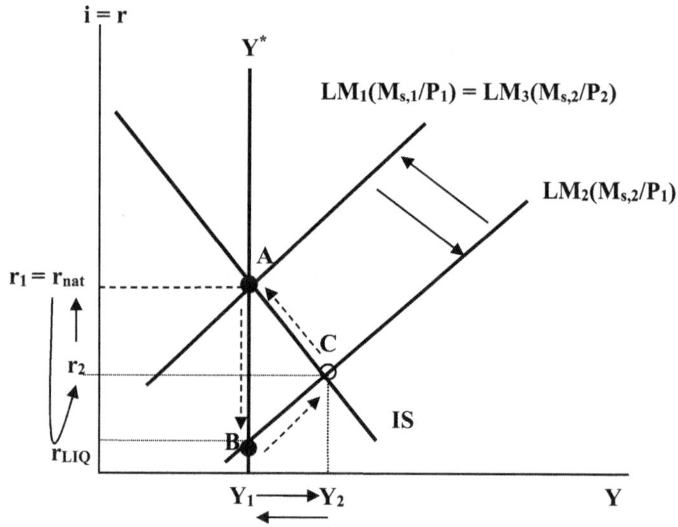

Fig. 6.9 Monetary expansion and the reversion of the interest rate in standard theory

supply; in particular, it does not distinguish between a one-off increase in the money supply and a rise in the growth rate of the money supply. In what follows, the four effects are explicitly separated. Figure 6.9 shows three of them.

At point A, the output is at the potential level ($Y_1 = Y^*$) and the market interest rate equals the natural rate ($r_1 = r_{nat}$), which is defined in New Keynesian literature as the intersection of the IS curve and the potential product Y^* (Woodford, 2003). Suppose that both the actual and expected inflation rates are zero, so that the nominal interest rate equals the real interest rate ($i = r$). The price level is assumed to be constant at P_1, so an expansion in the nominal money supply is reflected in a larger real money supply. In the first round, increasing the nominal money supply from $M_{S,1}$ to $M_{S,2}$, and consequently the real money supply from $M_{S,1}/P_1$ to $M_{S,2}/P_1$, lowers the interest rate. This is known as the liquidity effect (Gibson, 1970), and is reflected in the movement from point A to point B ($r_{LIQ} < r_1 = r_{nat}$) in Fig. 6.9. This reduction may support investment spending and subsequently the output of the economy.

The resulting higher incomes increase the demand for money, which may raise the interest rate. This is known as the income effect. It partly reduces the increase in investment spending. However, the output is still larger than before the shock, as shown by comparing points C and A. The partial reversion of the interest rate therefore comes from the money market, and it is consistent with the liquidity preference theory. At point C, the interest rate is below the natural level ($r_2 < r_1 = r_{\text{nat}}$) and the output exceeds the potential ($Y_2 > Y_1 = Y^*$). At this point, mainstream economics is in harmony with Austrian business cycle theory. Both theories predict that monetary expansion lowers the interest rate below the natural level and triggers an unsustainable boom. However, the channels are different. In mainstream economics, the impact on capital structure is largely ignored, and emphasis is instead placed on aggregate demand, the money market, and non-specific labour markets.

According to Wicksell (1936), a negative interest rate gap ($r_2 < r_1 = r_{\text{nat}}$) should lead to an increase in the price level. This conclusion is consistent with modern theory, which predicts that, in the long run, a positive output gap ($Y_2 > Y_1 = Y^*$) should result in a higher price level. In the third step, the price level rises from P_1 to P_2, which reduces the real money supply from $M_{S,2}/P_1$ to $M_{S,2}/P_2$. The LM curve shifts back to its original position along with the reversion of the real money supply, where $\text{LM}_3(M_{S,2}/P_2) = \text{LM}_1(M_{S,1}/P_1)$, and $M_{S,2}/P_2 = M_{S,1}/P_1 < M_{S,2}/P_1$. Output returns to its potential level, and the market interest rate reverts to the natural level. According to mainstream economics, money should be neutral in the long run, leaving real variables unaffected.

The third effect, which moves the interest rate from r_2 back to its natural level, can be called the price level effect. It is again derived from the money market, because the real money supply declines (or the nominal demand for money rises) due to a higher price level. This theory is consistent with Fig. 6.7, even though it relies on the Keynesian liquidity preference theory. The real sector is represented by the IS curve, Y^* curve, and the natural rate of interest. The IS-LM-Y^* model thus integrates the real and monetary sectors of the economy.

The problem of a constantly rising price level is not reflected here, because the model does not take the dynamics of the money supply into account. If the growth rate, and not only the level, of the money supply increases and causes a rise in both actual and expected inflation rates, the fourth effect—the Fisher effect—may arise. However, its inclusion separates the interest rate for the LM curve, which is constructed for the

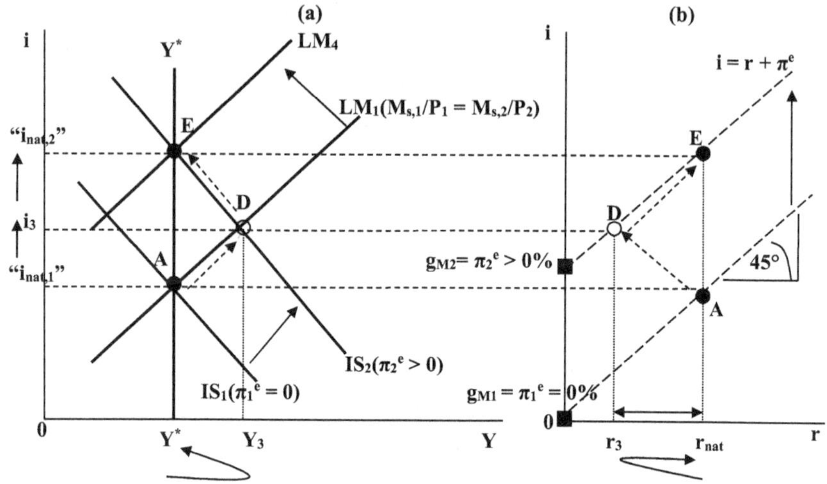

Fig. 6.10 Permanent increase in the money supply growth and the Fisher effect

money market and the nominal interest rate i, and the IS curve, which is derived from the goods market and the real interest rate r.

The money supply growing constantly ($M_{S,1} < M_{S,2} < M_{S,3} \ldots; g_{M2} > 0\%$) at the same rate as the price level ($P_1 < P_2 < P_3 \ldots; \pi_2 = \pi_2^e = g_{M2} > 0\%$) fixes the position of the LM curve ($M_{S,1}/P_1 = M_{S,2}/P_2 = \ldots$). The IS curve shifts outwards due to higher expected inflation ($\pi^e > 0$), which reduces the real interest rate for a given level of the nominal interest rate. Figure 6.10 indicates a period of booming economy ($Y_3 > Y^*$ in panel (a); $r_3 < r_{nat}$ in panel (b)), in which the Mundell-Tobin effect (Mundell, 1963; Tobin 1965) is active (point D) because the positive inflation rate and the resulting higher nominal interest rate lead to lower real demand for money, a lower real interest rate, and greater output.

Point D is consistent with the analysis in Fig. 6.8, which cannot be the ultimate equilibrium of the economy. In the long run, the output ends at the initial real potential level, and the market real interest rate at the natural rate (point E). The movement from point D to E is accompanied by an additional increase in the price level. Ultimately, the nominal interest rate is higher ("$i_{nat,2}$" > "$i_{nat,1}$") and, consequently, the real demand for money is lower. Thus, permanent monetary expansion ($g_{M2} > g_{M1} = 0\%$) reduces one real variable—real money balances. This decrease was caused by a temporarily higher inflation rate, which exceeded the expansion in the money supply.[14] Money is not super-neutral; it is only neutral in the long run.

This analysis may resolve the puzzle of interest-rate reversion indicated in Figs. 6.7 and 6.8, which were based on the price-level changes. A distinction must be made between the price-level effect, which is the outcome of a one-off increase in the money supply, and the Fisher effect, which results from a constantly rising money supply. However, this analysis relies heavily on liquidity preference theory, because all reversion processes come from an increase in the demand for money. As such, interest is considered a monetary rather than a real phenomenon, even though the long-run equilibrium of the economy is at point E, where the real interest rate is at the initial natural level, which is solely determined by real forces. However, this analysis lacks an examination of the capital structure and the relative prices between consumption goods and capital goods.

The Austrian analysis therefore requires one more element to explain the increase in the interest rate during the reversion process initiated by monetary expansion. This critical element is the growth in consumer demand at the end of the economic boom. The increase in demand leads to depletion of forced savings and the return of price margins (P_c/P_i) to their initial level. At this moment, the economy starts to suffer from lower saving. Artificially initiated capital structures cannot be completed, because resources are attracted back to stages closer to final consumption. As emphasized earlier, the more important factor is the dynamics of relative prices (in this case P_c/P_i) rather than the movement of the general price level. The interest-rate reversion process that could explain Austrian theory is shown in Figs. 6.11 and 6.12.

An alternative graphical representation of the interest-rate reversion can be based on the principles in Hayek (1937). Entrepreneurs, misled by the fall in the interest rate, expect a sufficient amount of real savings to be present in the future. As discussed, monetary expansion cannot permanently guarantee this inflow. The relative lack of real saving therefore results in an increase in the interest rate, which will overshoot the level

[14] If real demand for money were not sensitive to the nominal interest rate, the LM curve would be vertical, and the economy might move smoothly to a higher interest rate without a boom period. In such a case, there would be no period with a temporarily higher inflation rate, which would be perfectly equal to the rate of monetary expansion in all periods. Money would be super-neutral in the long run.

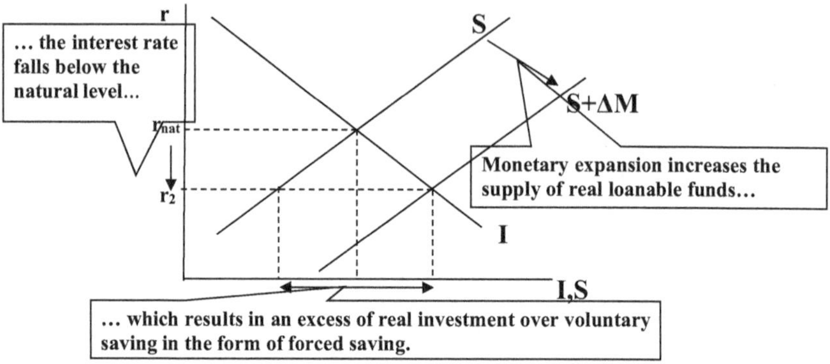

Fig. 6.11 Dynamics of the interest rate in Austrian business cycle theory (I)

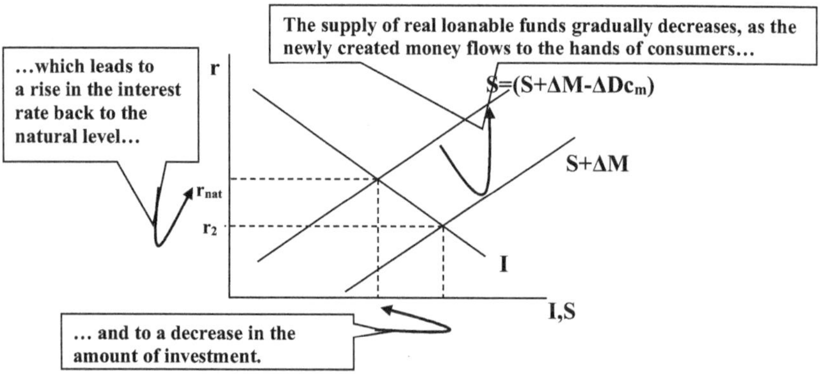

Fig. 6.12 Dynamics of the interest rate in Austrian business cycle theory (II)

that would have been set in the market if a false signal in the form of an artificially lower interest rate had not been introduced. However, it is not immediately obvious why expectations about future real saving should be wrong. One possible explanation can be found in the monetary part of the economy. Changes in the money supply may disturb the critical signal to which entrepreneurs respond—the interest rate. This distorted signal, in turn, leads to the over-optimistic behaviour of entrepreneurs, which has insufficient support in the real economy.

In Fig. 6.13, the cut in the interest rate from r_e to r_2 caused by monetary expansion can be understood as price regulation that leads to an

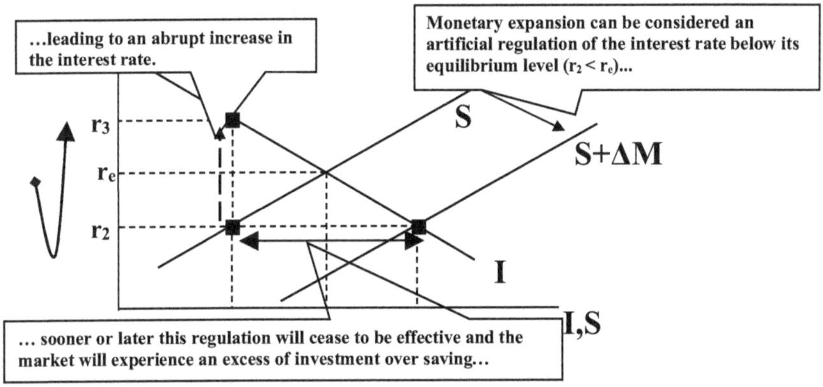

Fig. 6.13 Alternative representation of interest rate reversion

excess of investment over (voluntary) saving. Sooner or later, however, economic forces will be activated in the economy, which will ultimately render this intervention ineffective. The initial decline in the real interest rate will result in a drop in the amount of real saving, which will raise the interest rate to r_3.

For some economists, even this type of analysis may not be satisfactory. Especially the idea that growth in consumption and profitability should reduce investment may be seen as totally fantastic, at least for Keynesians. However, Austrian capital theory can offer answers.

If we accept the Keynesian argument that growing consumption demand and overall profitability increase investment, the implications in the Austrian model are as follows. The rise in investment will lead to the growth in the roundaboutness of production processes. The longer methods initiated require resources in the form of original means of production (labour, land), and also complementary variable capital, to be completed in the future. Assume that resources are scarce, which is especially reasonable at the top of the boom.[15] Resources can be allocated to early stages only at the expense of other stages of production—those that operate very close to final consumption. As a result, initiated capital structures begin to attract more resources from late stages. This shift will reduce the supply of present consumption goods, because new longer processes will provide them only in the distant future. Keynesian analysis leads to a paradoxical

[15] The situation with relative abundance of the factors of production is analysed in Chap. 8.

conclusion. An increase in consumer demand (i.e. demand for present goods) ultimately results in a reduction of the supply of consumption goods (i.e. the supply of present goods) because resources have been shifted to the production of future consumption goods.

It would be difficult to find a more significant failure of the market system. Moreover, if an increase in demand for consumption goods leads to a reduction in their supply, the overall process cannot be sustainable, as both tendencies push consumer goods prices upwards. With higher consumer prices, profit margins will skyrocket, because the P_c/P_i ratio will rise above all limits.[16]

Sooner or later, the whole process must be disrupted because very high profit margins and a deficient supply of present consumption goods will motivate entrepreneurs to move a considerable part of resources back to their production. Thus, an increase in consumer demand can never lead to sustainable growth of capital in the economy; it can never provoke a permanent lengthening of the Hayek triangle.[17]

This analysis suggests that Austrian theory has sufficient tools to disprove the traditional Keynesian idea. Furthermore, if we take the Keynesian argument *ad absurdum*, its fantastic content can be unmasked. As shown earlier, Keynesians assume that the increase in consumption demand should induce higher investment spending. As a result, factors of production are then attracted to the early stages of production, where they earn incomes for their services. It is reasonable to expect that new incomes will be used mainly for consumption. At the same time, however, only a small part of the processes initiated mature as final consumption goods. This must necessarily lead to an imbalance between supply and demand in the consumer goods market, a consequent rise in consumer prices, and, ultimately, higher profitability of stages that are very close to final consumption.

According to the Keynesian argument, the increase in profitability will lead to an additional rise in investment spending, which, in the Austrian model, results in further lengthening of the production structure. As a result, more and more factors of production will be attracted to processes that produce little or no final consumption goods in the near future. Using

[16] Since the resources are moving to early stages of production, P_i (i.e. the price of capital goods) falls, which will further encourage the growth of profit margins (P_c/P_i).

[17] This theory contradicts the concept of the accelerator, thoroughly investigated in Hayek (1939).

the argument ***reductio ad absurdum***, Keynesian analysis necessarily implies that the constantly rising demand for consumption goods leads to zero supply of these goods, which is impossible. This theory could only work if incomes earned by various factors of production, which were attracted to the early stages, were all completely saved (Hayek, 1935). However, no reasonable economic argument entitles us to assume that no part of the new income will be used for consumption. This is as inconceivable as the statement that an increase in consumer demand will provoke a permanent lengthening of the production structure.

Finally, we can propose one fundamental conclusion. An increase in consumption demand will always cause a partial destruction of capital in the economy, especially during the business cycle. The entire process is orchestrated by the interest rate, specifically by its reverse (U-shaped) dynamics.

The Dynamics of the Money Supply

Thus far, we have analysed the reversion process of the interest rate over the business cycle. The primary shock came from the monetary part of the economy—from the increase in the total money supply. Although not explicitly emphasized, we assumed that the primary increase was only a one-off shock to the money supply. This section considers what the dynamics of the interest rate will be if the central bank continues the monetary expansion.[18]

When upward interest rate movements are activated, continued monetary expansion may renew downward pressure. The crucial question is how much increase in the money supply is necessary to overcome the reverse dynamics of the interest rate and thereby to prevent shortening of the Hayek triangle, accompanied by the inevitable destruction of the capital structures that have been initiated. In other words, what amount of money flow is needed to complete artificially lengthened production processes? What is the necessary size of money injections that would generate new rounds of forced saving?

One relevant answer is that the same absolute rise in the quantity of money will suffice. For example, the series of the money supply would be 1000; 1100; 1200; 1300; and so on. Another possibility is that a constant growth rate of the money supply, for example 10%, will be adequate to

[18] Constant credit expansion is also analysed by Evans et al. (2022).

permanently reduce the interest rate, that is, 1000; 1100; 1210; 1331; and so forth. The third possibility is that the money supply must accelerate, that is, the growth rate would gradually increase, for example, from 3% to 4%, 5%; and so forth.

Since Austrian theory has never been developed into a rigorous mathematical model, it is relatively difficult to decide which answers may be correct. Hayek suggested that:

> *We shall now assume that it does so, not at a constant, absolute rate, but at such a rate as is necessary to maintain the increased volume of real investment. This will mean a constant percentage increase in the total flow (and quantity) of money, because, if before it needed a 1 per cent addition to attract the additional resources to investment, after the total money stream (and general prices) will have risen by 1 per cent, it will need an increase of 1.01 per cent to produce the same effect and so on.*
>
> Hayek (1969, p. 280)

If we accept Hayek's reasoning, the money supply must accelerate to keep the interest rate lower. This can be demonstrated in several diagrams. Figure 6.14 illustrates that the primary effect of the monetary injection ΔM_1 on the real interest rate is neutralized by a consequent increase in consumer demand $\Delta D_{c,m}$. To reduce the real interest rate again, a second-round injection, ΔM_2, is needed, which must sufficiently exceed the first.

Figure 6.15 depicts the same approach with the nominal interest rate i. If the central bank is determined to fix the nominal interest rate at an artificially lower level ($i_{CB} < i_1$), the inflationary process will start in the economy. As discussed earlier, nominal market interest rates tend to increase along with (expected) inflation due to the Fisher effect. This is reflected in shifts in both the investment and saving curves. The persistent upward pressure on the nominal interest rate forces the central bank to accelerate injections of money into the economy, which will further fuel price inflation. This diagram raises the well-known question of whether the central bank is able to control the nominal interest rate, or whether the interest rate is determined by real forces. [19]

[19] This question was emphasized, for example, by Friedman (1968). The new Keynesian literature also suggests that the central bank does not have complete freedom in setting the interest rate. It must follow the Taylor principle; otherwise, inflation will spiral out of control (Woodford 2003).

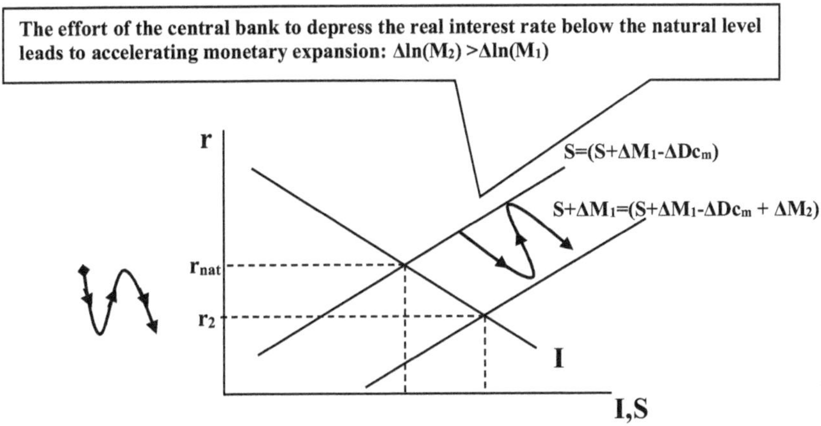

Fig. 6.14 Accelerating monetary expansion

One additional impulse must be noted in connection with this process. The steady flow of money into the economy will eventually exert strong demand pressure on consumer goods markets. Consequently, profit margins (P_c/P_i) will rise. If the central bank fixes the nominal interest rate and commercial banks follow the direction of the central bank, entrepreneurs are motivated to borrow money to make profits that arise in the form of differences between price margins in the production structure and the interest rate in the banking system. Through new loans created in the banking system, entrepreneurs are constantly acquiring new money, and the process reinforces itself. In the end, consumers obtain new money and spend it on final consumer goods. The whole process of rising consumer prices, increasing profit margins, and new loans for entrepreneurs may begin anew unless the central bank changes its monetary policy by imposing a sufficient interest-rate hike to stop the inflationary spiral. This approach is sketched in Fig. 6.16.

In Fig. 6.15 we encounter the endogenous money supply, which we discuss in more detail in Chap. 7. At this stage, however, it can be concluded that monetary forces can never surpass forces arising in the real economy. The real forces eventually reverse the movement triggered by the monetary impulse. Hayek wrote in this context:

Fig. 6.15 Accelerating monetary expansion and the Fisher effect

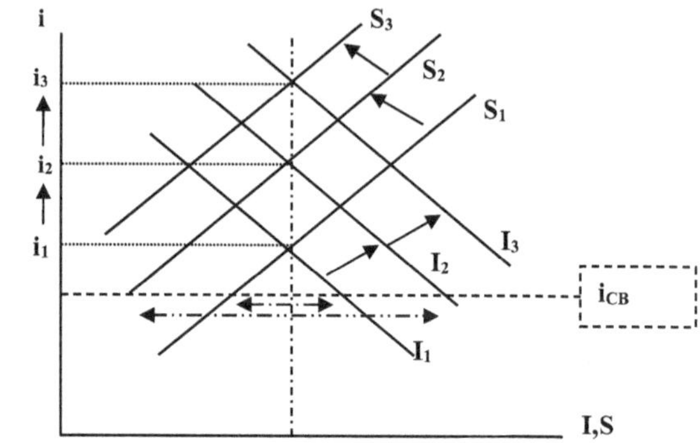

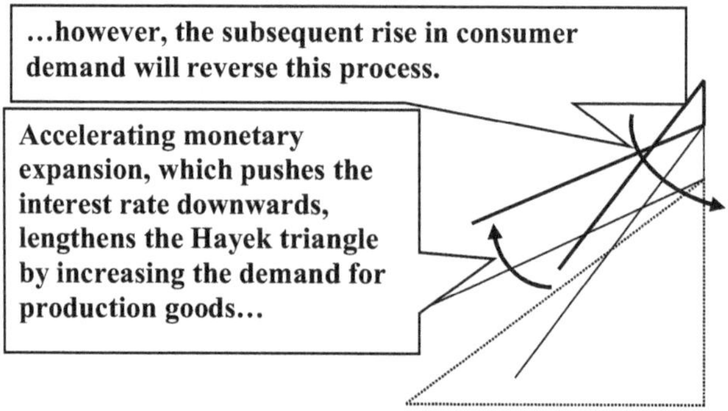

Fig. 6.16 Hayek triangle and accelerating monetary expansion

> *As we have seen, any delay by monetary means of the adjustments made necessary by real changes can only have the effect of further accentuating these real changes, and any purely monetary change which in the first instance deflects interest rates in one direction is bound to set up forces which will ultimately change them in the opposite direction.*
> Hayek (1941, p. 393)

The last issue examined in this section is the extent to which the money supply can eventually rise. Today, most central banks explicitly or implicitly target inflation, and price stability is officially among their primary objectives. Within this framework, the central bank is forced to raise the interest rate to stop the inflationary process and to cool off the economy, even at the cost of a severe recession. However, it would be a serious mistake to think that the cause of a recession is a tightening of monetary policy. Careful analysis would instead suggest that the primary source of the consequent recession is inadequate interest rate manipulation, which initiated an economic boom. The subsequent rise in the interest rate is only a necessary reaction if the economy is not to end in a hyperinflationary disaster.

Consider a framework in which no brake is applied to eventually stop the accelerating flow of money into the economy. Can the Hayek triangle be permanently lengthened? In other words, can constantly rising monetary expansion indefinitely support the extended capital structure by creating an undying source of forced saving? Obviously, the answer can hardly be yes, because the final limit is the total collapse of the currency. A hyperinflationary catastrophe is often highlighted by Mises (1996) and Rothbard (2004), but Hayek also raised a similar question:

> *It has always been an open question to me as to how long a process of continued inflation, not checked by a built-in limit on the supply of money and credit, could effectively maintain investment above the volume justified by the voluntary rate of savings. It may well be that this inevitable check only comes when inflation becomes so rampant-as the progressively higher rate of inflation required to maintain a given volume of investment must make it sooner or later-that money ceases to be an adequate accounting basis.*
> Hayek (1969, p. 282)

However, many forces can be detected that will undoubtedly block ongoing lengthening of the production structure long before the ultimate collapse of the currency. The first brake is the increasing risk premium, which usually arises during galloping inflation. It discourages long-term investment in favour of shorter-term investment. Shorter production techniques are then preferred over roundabout methods, even if the inflow of money into the system continues. Higher inflation can also generate fictitious profits, when firms keep their accounting books in historical costs and do not correctly revalue their capital, undermining the real value of capital depreciation. In such a case, firms acting upon misleading information about nominal profits consume part of their capital instead of maintaining it intact.

Even if we overlook the risk premium and the historical-cost accounting, one strong impulse for capital destruction will undoubtedly emerge when the inflation rate reaches relatively high levels. Thus far, we have analysed the dynamics of the money supply. However, economic disturbances can also be caused by changes in the demand for money. When prices are rapidly rising, it is reasonable to assume that people will reduce their real money balances, which are eroded by high inflation rates. Reduced real money balances can then expand consumer demand. The late stages of production will face another source of demand, which will raise their profitability. This can stop the lengthening of the capital structure as resources are attracted back to the consumption stages, even when monetary expansion constantly feeds demand in the early stages. In other words, accelerating monetary expansion may change the attitudes of people to holding money. By reducing the optimum level of their real money balances, people may further reinforce total consumption demand, which will eliminate part of the capital stock in the economy. As a result, even accelerating monetary expansion cannot suppress the reversion dynamics of the interest rate.

References

Cowen, T. (1997). *Risk and Business Cycles: New and Old Austrian Perspectives.* Routledge.

Coyne, C. J., & Boettke, P. J. (2020). *The Essential Austrian Economics.* Fraser Institute.

Evans, A. J., Cachanosky, N., & Thorpe, R. (2022). The Upper Turning Point in the Austrian Business Cycle Theory. *The Review of Austrian Economics, 35*, 89–97.

Fisher, I. (1930). *Theory of Interest.* The Macmillan Company.

Friedman, M. (1968). The Role of Monetary Policy. *The American Economic Review, 58*(1), 1–17.

Garrison, R. W. (2001). *Time and Money, The Macroeconomics of Capital Structure.* Routledge.

Gibson, W. E. (1970). The Lag in the Effect of Monetary Policy on Income and Interest Rates. *The Quarterly Journal of Economics, 84*(2), 288–300.

Horwitz, S. (2016). Hayek on the Neutrality of Money. In S. Horwitz (Ed.), *Studies in Austrian Macroeconomics, Advances in Austrian Economics, Volume 20.* Emerald Group Publishing Limited.

Kaldor, N. (1942). Professor Hayek and the Concertina-Effect. *Economica, 9*(36), 359–382.

Klausinger, H. (2011). Hayek and Kaldor: Close Encounter at LSE. *History of Economic Ideas, 19*(3), 135–163.

Mankiw, N. G., & Romer, D. (Eds.). (1991a). *New Keynesian Economics: Volume 1.* MIT Press.

Mankiw, N. G., & Romer, D. (Eds.). (1991b). *New Keynesian Economics.* MIT Press.

Moss, L. S., & Vaughn, K. I. (2010). Hayek's Ricardo Effect: A Second Look. *The American Journal of Economics and Sociology, 69*(1), 333–358.
Mundell, R. A. (1963). Inflation and Real Interest. *Journal of Political Economy, 71*(3), 280–283.
O'Driscoll, G. P., Jr., & Rizzo, M. J. (1996). *The Economics of Time and Ignorance* (2nd ed.). Routledge.
Potuzak, P. (2016). *Hayek MV-Rule*. Elsevier. Retrieved from SSRN: https://ssrn.com/abstract=2857719
Potuzak, P. (2017). *The Hayek-Taylor Rule*. Elsevier. Retrieved from SSRN: https://ssrn.com/abstract=2972121
Potuzak, P. (2018). Price Level Stabilization: Hayek Contra Mainstream Economics. *Prague Economic Papers, 27*(4), 449–478.
Rothbard, M. N. (2004 [1962]). *Man, Economy, and State*. Ludwig von Mises Institute.
Sraffa, P. (1932). Dr. Hayek on Money and Capital. *The Economic Journal, 42*(165), 42–53.
Tobin, J. (1965). Money and Economic Growth. *Econometrica, 33*(4), 671–684.
van Zijp, R. (1992). *Austrian and New Classical Business Cycle Theories*. Tinbergen Institute Research Series.
von Hayek, F. A. (1933 [1929]). *Monetary Theory and the Trade Cycle*. Jonathan Cape.
von Hayek, F. A. (1935 [1931]). *Prices and Production* (2nd ed.). Augustus M. Kelly.
von Hayek, F. A. (1937). Investment that Raises the Demand for Capital. *The Review of Economic Statistics, 19*(4), 174–177.
von Hayek, F. A. (1939). *Profits, Interest and Investment*. George Routledge & Sons Ltd..
von Hayek, F. A. (1941). *The Pure Theory of Capital*. The University of Chicago Press.
von Hayek, F. A. (1942a). The Ricardo Effect. *Economica, 9*(34), 127–152.
von Hayek, F. A. (1942b). [Professor Hayek and the Concertina-Effect]: A Comment. *Economica, 9*(36), 383–385.
von Hayek, F. A. (1969). Three Elucidations of the Ricardo Effect. *The Journal of Political Economy, 77*(2), 274–285.
von Mises, L. (1996 [1949]). *Human Action: A Treatise on Economics* (4th ed.). Fox & Wilkes.
von Mises, L. (2009 [1912]). *Theory of Money and Credit*. Ludwig von Mises Institute.
White, L. H. (1999). Hayek's Monetary Theory and Policy: A Critical Reconstruction. *Journal of Money, Credit and Banking, 31*(1), 109–120.
Wicksell, K. (1936 [1898]). *Interest and Prices*. Augustus M. Kelley.
Woodford, M. (2003). *Interest and Prices: Foundations of a Theory of Monetary Policy*. Princeton University Press.

CHAPTER 7

Further Dynamics of the Interest Rate in Austrian Theory

We assumed that the initial impulse for the business cycle and the subsequent interest rate dynamics should be sought in the behaviour of the central bank and monetary policy as such, especially in lowering the interest rate below the natural level. This approach, emphasized by Mises (1996) and Rothbard (2004), is modified in this chapter. Specifically, we examine a different evolution of the interest rate that can also be observed over the business cycle.

Hayek (1933) admitted that the initial impulse for the business cycle may arise in the real economy. Following his reasoning, assume that the economy is hit by a positive technological shock, the modern analytical counterpart of the older assumption of an invention that appears in the economy.

In the Böhm-Bawerk theory, the invention can further improve the technical superiority of present goods over future goods and make the time shape of the income stream steeper (Fisher, 1930). Both will increase the value premium of present goods over future goods. In the well-known Fisherian analysis, the invention increases investment opportunities in the

P. Potuzak, *Austrian Theory of Capital and Business Cycle*,
https://doi.org/10.1007/978-3-031-18728-5_7

Fig. 7.1 Positive technological shock in the loanable funds market

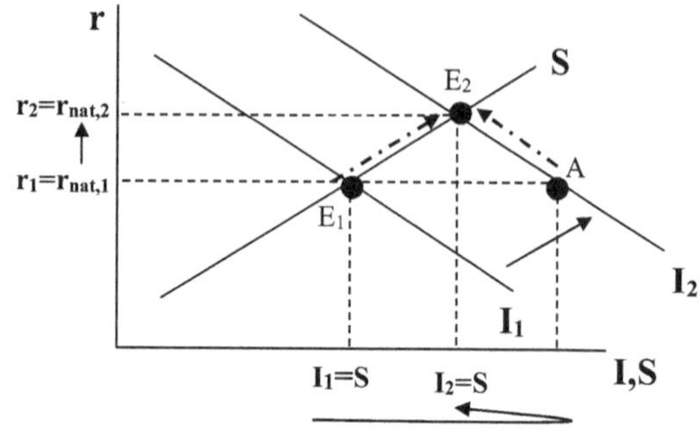

economy, which will raise the natural rate of interest for several periods.[1] Hayek (1941) follows the Fisherian or even Knightian analysis, by emphasizing the importance of the marginal product of capital, which is defined in Austrian theory as the additional final output of consumption goods that results from a marginal increase in the roundaboutness of the production process. Thus, a positive technological shock, or invention, shifts the curve of the marginal product of capital outwards.

In the loanable funds market, this improvement will be reflected in an outward shift of the investment curve. For a given shape of the saving curve, the natural rate of interest must increase. According to Hayek (1933), if no reaction is activated in the monetary part of the economy, there is no reason to expect that the business cycle should be triggered, because voluntary saving is consistent with higher investment.[2]

[1] The subsequent dynamics of the natural rate of interest is more complicated than the path suggested in this chapter. The invention causes an increase in output and incomes, and consequently savings, that will push the interest rate down. However, a precise description of the path of the natural interest rate would require a more complex model of growth theory. Fisher (1930) himself proposed that the eventual level of the interest rate would be somewhat lower. In contrast, modern growth models, such as Solow or Ramsey-Cass-Koopmans models, base their predictions on whether the initial shock improves only the level of technologies in the economy, or also their growth rate.

[2] Pure time preference theory (PTPT) advocated by Mises and Rothbard rejects that the natural rate of interest is affected by the productivity of capital. PTPT is discussed in Potuzak (2016a, 2016b, 2016c). Rothbard ([1963] 2000, p. 32) states:

In defense of the Mises "anti-bank" position, we must first point out that the natural interest rate or "profit rate" does not suddenly increase because of vague improvements in "investment opportunities." The natural rate increases because time preferences increase.

As shown in Fig. 7.1, the initial market and natural rate of interest ($r_1 = r_{nat,1}$) are no longer consistent with the equilibrium in the loanable funds market. At this level, investment exceeds voluntary saving. To clear the market, the market interest rate must increase from r_1 to r_2. It will follow the path of the natural rate of interest. The increase would be more significant for a steeper saving curve.

As the market interest rate rises, two phenomena begin to work. First, part of the investment is eliminated (moving from point A to E_2) because only the most profitable projects can survive at a higher interest rate. Second, a higher interest rate attracts new voluntary saving (from point E_1 to E_2). Compared to the state before the invention, more investment projects are initiated. Their number depends on the willingness of people to give up present consumption.

It could be puzzling to illustrate this change in the natural interest rate in the Hayek triangle, because the triangle was designed primarily to depict changes in the saving rate. However, as the interest rate rises, the triangle becomes steeper. It is reasonable to assume that, with a given amount of primary factors of production, the invention allows a given output of consumption goods to be produced more rapidly than before. Hence, the triangle also becomes shorter.[3] If the saving curve were perfectly inelastic, in other words, if the increase in the interest rate did not persuade people to postpone their consumption, a positive technological shock would transform the Hayek triangle, as shown in Fig. 7.2. In contrast, if people respond to changes in the interest rate, its increase will reduce their present consumption, which allows for a partial rise in the roundaboutness of the production process depicted in Fig. 7.3.

Fig. 7.2 Positive technological shock with perfectly inelastic saving curve—the Hayek triangle representation

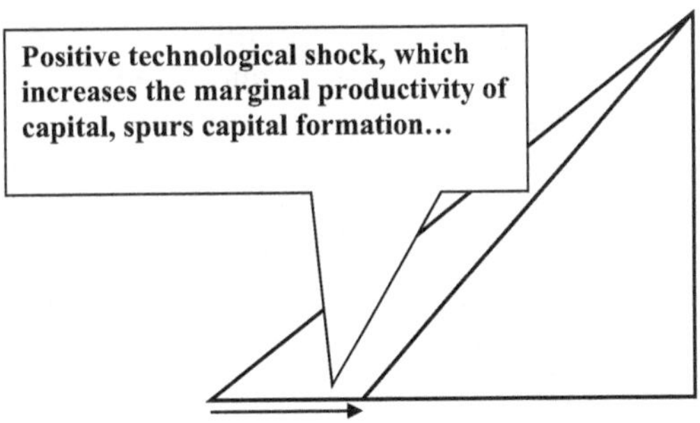

[3]This change in the shape of the triangle can be deduced from Hayek (1941, 1942).

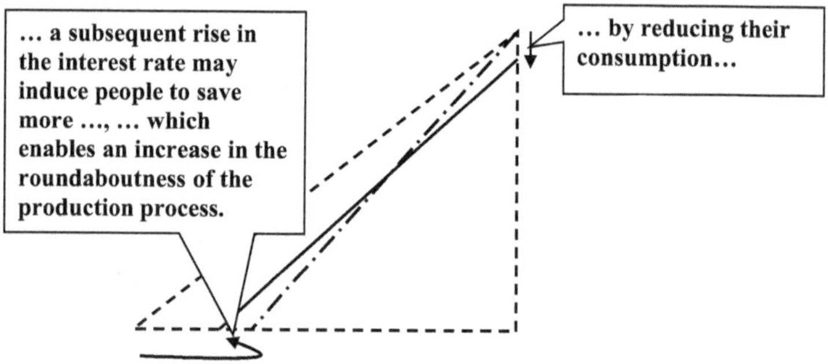

Fig. 7.3 Positive technological shock with elastic saving curve—the Hayek triangle representation

In Chap. 2, the greater productivity of longer methods was also explained by noting that some inventions cannot be used with shorter methods due to insufficient savings. These inventions were termed endogenous because they were present in the economy, but were not used due to a lack of capital. In other words, it was understood that longer techniques that apply better technology can increase output of consumption goods; however, these methods require more time. In contrast, the technological shock presented in Figs. 7.1 and 7.2 arises "outside the economy". This new technology was not known before and allows the production time to shorten, speeding the production process, so that consumption goods can mature sooner. This invention can be called exogenous.

This analysis suggests that a positive technological shock raises the natural rate of interest. However, the model deliberately disregarded the monetary part of the economy. In the real world, saving and investment are traded in the form of money. Can we assume that money plays no significant role in this transmission? In other words, will the response of the banking sector to the increase in the natural interest rate be purely neutral? Will the banking system follow the evolution of the natural rate of interest by increasing market interest rates?

Figure 7.4 shows two possible responses of the banking system to an increase in the natural rate of interest. This scheme depicts a simplified balance sheet of commercial banks that initially hold a 100% reserve ratio. In situation (a), banks hold 100 in reserves to fully cover demand deposits, while loans of 200 are financed by time (term) deposits that clients cannot

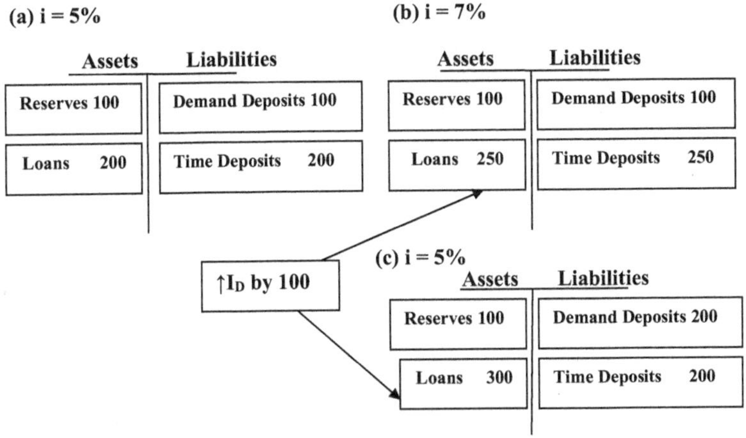

Fig. 7.4 Endogeneity of money in the Austrian model

withdraw immediately.[4] This situation can also be interpreted as follows: Investment is financed by voluntary saving, and the market interest rate is equal to the natural level, which is, for example, 5%.

Consider a positive technological shock that increases investment demand and the natural interest rate from 5% to 7%. This shock also leads to greater demand for loans in the banking sector (e.g. from 200 to 300). At this stage, demand for 300 exceeds the supply of 200, and the interest rate in the banking sector should rise. If this happens (situation b), part of the investment demand is eliminated (e.g. from 300 it becomes 250), and some savings are likely to be attracted (from 200 to 250). Clearly, voluntary saving is again in balance with investment. This equilibrium was enabled by increasing the market interest rate from 5% to 7%. The market interest rate is also equal to the new natural interest rate.

However, a different response from the banking sector is conceivable. Assume that the banking sector keeps the market interest rate unaltered and fully accommodates the increased demand for loans by creating new demand deposits (situation c). In this case, the phenomenon of forced saving emerges, because the investment (300) exceeds the voluntary savings (200), and the market interest rate (5%) does not keep pace with its

[4] For simplicity, we assume that the time structure of loans and time deposits is perfectly matched.

natural counterpart (7%).[5] The imbalance between voluntary saving and investment is possible due to the elastic money supply, which increases from 100 to 200, as banks cease to hold 100% reserves. The reserve-deposit ratio falls from 100% to 50% (= 100/200). A maturity mismatch arises in the banking system, because long-term loans are partly financed by demand deposits that can be withdrawn immediately.[6]

Clearly, in situation (c) in Fig. 7.4, the market interest rate fails to transmit information about the increase in investment demand and the higher natural interest rate. It would be surprising if this failure had no repercussions in the real economy.

We have analysed two extreme responses of the banking sector. In the real world, the reaction can occur at any point in this hypothetical interval. Hayek (1933) assumed that when demand for loans increases, commercial banks would rarely raise their interest rates sufficiently high and fast enough. Their typical response is much closer to situation (c), as they increase their lending capacity rather than interest rates. If some banks do not offer new loans during the general expansion in credit, they will accumulate more reserves from other banks. In addition, only an increase in the interest rate can weaken rising demand for credit. However, such a strategy puts conservative banks at a competitive disadvantage with other banks, which have reduced the reserve ratio and expanded lending to entrepreneurs. The accumulation of reserves and competition from other banks may persuade more conservative banks to follow the "mainstream" behaviour. As a result, credit expansion will become universal, and the market interest rate will remain below the natural level.

So far, we have disregarded the response of the central bank. It is not very far-fetched to assume that the central bank will reinforce rather than dampen the entire process. Because central banks fix their interest rates at a predetermined level, commercial banks can keep their reserve ratio intact simply by borrowing high-powered money directly from the central bank.

[5] This example is highly stylized. One major inconsistency lies in the fact that investment and saving are flows, whereas monetary and credit aggregates are stocks. It would be more in line with the concept of flows if we assumed that the investment demand increased to 100, and part of this demand (e.g. 50) was reduced due to a higher interest rate. Similar reasoning would hold for saving. A more detailed analysis of the money creation process can be found in Huerta de Soto ([1998] 2006).

[6] Maturity mismatch is discussed, for example, by Bagus (2010), Bagus and Howden (2010), and Barnett and Block (2009). Fractional reserves are analysed, for example, by Selgin and White (1996).

As a result, the increased demand for loans is transmitted through the banking system to the central bank, which eventually supports credit expansion.

Although the central bank may follow a certain policy rule when setting policy rates, the greatest weight is usually given to inflation and output gaps, not to credit or monetary aggregates. Because only these aggregates provide crucial information that the demand for loans has intensified, it would require enormous accuracy in the central bank forecasts to discover that the natural interest rate has risen.[7] We will show that the output gap and higher inflation are more the result of the whole process. Both arose mainly due to the inability of the central bank to keep track of the natural interest rate. In other words, raising policy rates after positive output and inflation gaps have opened is too late for the central bank to stop the course of events known as the business cycle.

It is therefore reasonable to assume that, in the current banking and monetary system, the market interest rate does not sufficiently respond to an increase in the natural interest rate, either due to the accommodative behaviour of commercial banks, or because of a delay in the monetary policy response. The consequent interest rate dynamics can be illustrated in the following set of figures. A positive technological shock shifts investment demand outwards. For simplicity, Fig. 7.5 assumes that the saving curve is vertical. At a given market interest rate r_1, higher investment demand is fully satisfied by the inflow of money from the banking sector. At this stage, it is not important whether the primary source of the newly

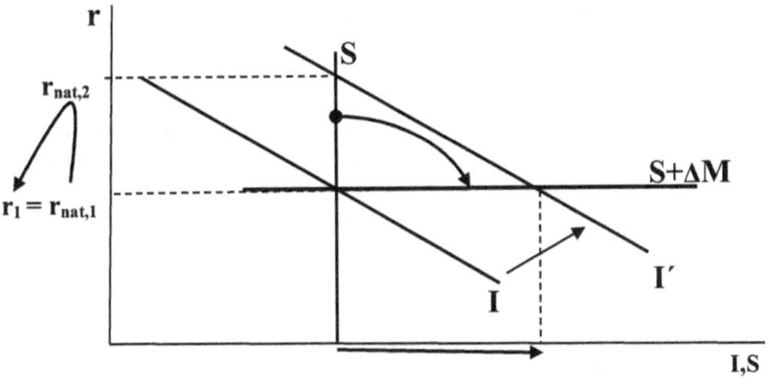

Fig. 7.5 Endogeneity of money in the loanable funds market

[7] A similar idea can be found in Cassel (1928, p. 528).

injected money is the central bank, commercial banks, or both. The crucial fact is that part of the investment is financed by newly created money rather than by voluntary saving.

Figure 7.5 shows that the natural rate of interest $r_{nat,2}$ exceeds the market rate r_1. This is equivalent to the statement that forced saving has emerged in the economy, which allows the capital structure in Fig. 7.6 to be artificially lengthened. It should be absolutely clear that the business cycle process has been triggered. The production structure is artificially longer because more has been invested than is justified by voluntary saving. The only difference in contrast to the benchmark analysis in Figs. 5.1 and 5.2 from Chap. 5 is that the money supply is endogenous rather than exogenous, because the banking system sets the interest rate and fully accommodates the greater demand for credit.

Cochran and Call (2000) emphasize that the economic boom in the process described earlier is peculiar.[8] It contains two components that are indistinguishable in official statistics, but Austrian theory can disentangle them. The first part of the faster economic growth can be attributed to the positive technological shock (invention) and can be considered sound. The second part was provoked by artificial credit expansion, which accommodated the increased demand for loans, and is not supported by voluntary saving. This part of the boom is unsound. The economy is therefore

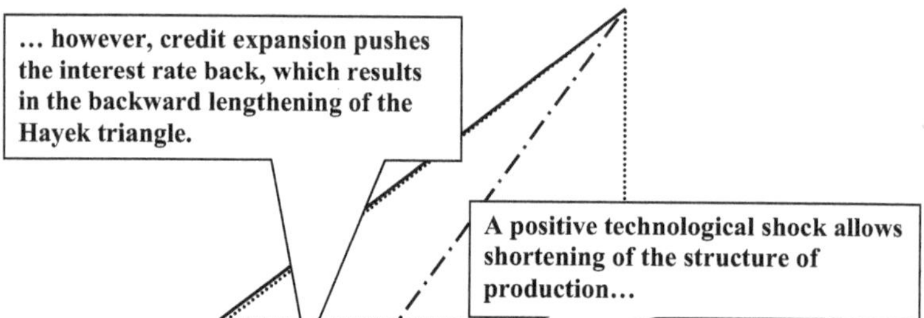

Fig. 7.6 Investment demand being accommodated by the injection of money—Hayek triangle representation

[8] More on this can also be found in Cochran and Call (1998), Cochran et al. (1999, 2003), and Cochran (2004).

growing faster than it would without the inflow of money into the system. This analysis seems to be consistent with official statistics on economic booms, which report above-average investment in this phase of the business cycle. Austrian theory predicts similar behaviour because credit expansion is channelled primarily to the creation of new capital structures, as the largest demand for loans comes from sectors where the marginal product of capital increases.[9]

As analysed in previous sections, the artificial part of the economic boom cannot be maintained forever. Sooner or later, the newly created money will end up in the hands of consumers. This will terminate the forced saving source of lengthening of the capital structure in the economy. Resources will be attracted back to the consumption stages, and new capital structures will never be completed. This phase of the business cycle also appears to be consistent with data, suggesting that investment spending collapses to some degree in recessions. The Austrian model offers the same prediction.

The crucial source of the capital shortening lies in the dynamics of the market interest rate, which will gradually increase to a higher natural level. Only another round of credit expansion can overturn this trend. However, it would be rather surprising if the central bank did not play a significant role in this process. Increased demand for cash is usually observed in booms, so banks that have been exposed to a lower reserve-deposit ratio due to credit expansion will find it difficult to continue this policy without central bank support. In other words, a relaxed monetary policy is required to sustain credit expansion. Otherwise, commercial banks should stop granting new loans, as their exposure would be too fragile. At this point, only accelerating credit expansion can keep the market interest rate below the natural level. Therefore, if the central bank raises its interest rate, commercial banks will follow this policy, and the boom will be terminated. The long-run consequences of credit expansion are depicted in Figs. 7.7 and 7.8.

We have demonstrated that technology-driven economic growth can end in a painful recession if the initial boom was exacerbated by an inflow of money from the banking system, which insufficiently raised interest

[9] The Austrian analysis should be distinguished from real business cycle theory. King and Plosser (1984), for example, conclude that the expansion of deposits during an economic boom is only a neutral response of the banking sector to a positive technological shock.

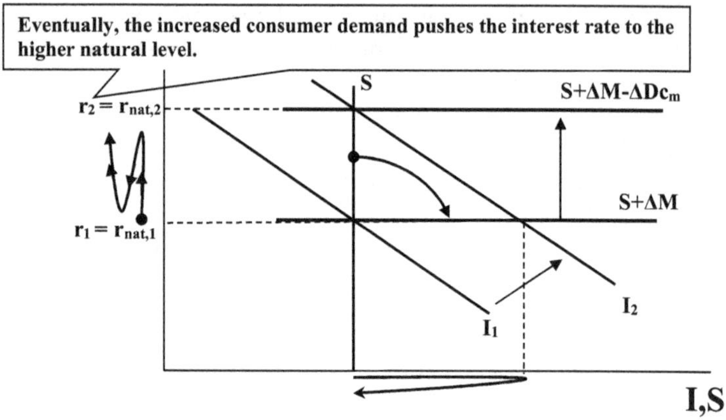

Fig. 7.7 The reverse dynamics of the interest rate

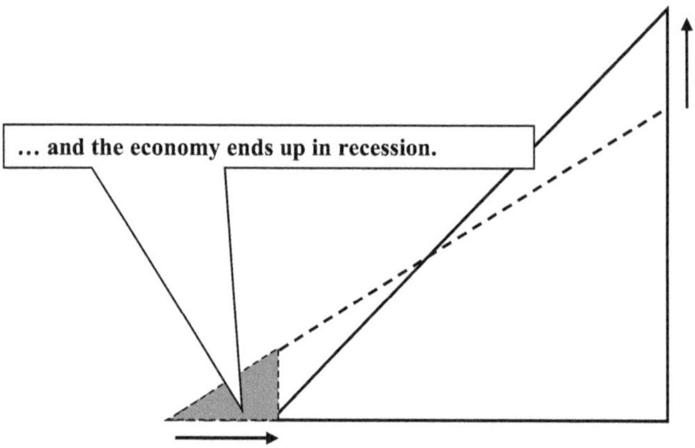

Fig. 7.8 Eventual recession

rates as investment demand increased. At the same time, it is extremely difficult for monetary authorities to detect from official statistics that growing output is not sustainable. Their own (in)activity can be a source of this unsustainability even if their interest rate policy is considered passive.

Demand for Money and the Interest Rate

Analysis of one more interest-rate dynamics remains, which can be found in one of Hayek's (1941) most complex books. Consider again a positive technological shock. This time, assume that both the amount of savings and the quantity of money in the economy are fixed. The central bank not only holds the monetary base constant, but the entire super-structure of deposits set up by commercial banks remains unchanged.

A positive technological shock shifts the investment curve outwards and raises the natural rate of interest. Because we assume a vertical saving curve and a fixed amount of money, the amount of investment cannot increase, and the growth of the marginal product of capital will only result in a higher market (and natural) interest rate.

However, there may be one important source that will allow entrepreneurs to increase the amount of resources at their command, which was mentioned in the analysis of the limits of monetary expansion in lengthening the production structure in Chap. 6. New investment can also be financed from real money balances held by people. In this case, it is critical to distinguish between saving, which represents part of the flow of income that has not been consumed, and money balances, which represent the most liquid part of the stock of assets accumulated by households over a certain period of time. Money balances as a stock can be increased by reducing the flow of consumption or the flow of saving. In contrast, either flow can be raised without decreasing the second flow, when people dissolve part of their money balances.

As a result, money balances can finance increased investment spending when the money supply is fixed and people are reluctant to reduce their present consumption. As noted earlier, a positive technological shock raises the interest rate. If the demand for money is sufficiently elastic with respect to the interest rate, people may rearrange their asset portfolios by reducing their money balances. By buying interest-bearing assets without decreasing present consumption, people transfer part of their money balances to entrepreneurs who offer higher interest rates. This stream of money allows firms to attract resources, and the capital structure can be lengthened.

It is important to realize that as the demand for money declines, the demand for consumption goods is not necessarily reduced. This situation is therefore similar to pure credit expansion. Investment spending increases even though the demand for consumer goods remains unchanged. The early stages of production then attract resources. If there are no idle factors of production in the economy, they can only be obtained at the expense of stages that are close to final consumption. Forced saving arises even in this situation, although it is quite inaccurate to call this saving "forced". It is the result of people's voluntary decisions rather than manipulation of the money supply. In the monetary economy, money is a "loose joint" that can create an imbalance between investment and saving (Hayek, 1941, p. 408). This imbalance can arise due to changes in not only the money supply, but also the demand for money.[10]

This situation is similar to the theory analysed in Figs. 7.5 and 7.6. The only difference is that the excess of investment over saving is financed by the released money balances rather than by monetary expansion. However, the economy must undergo a series of events that resemble the business cycle. The higher velocity of money, rather than a larger money supply, initiates more roundabout methods at the expense of the production of final consumer goods. In the end, money is earned by the original factors of production (mainly labour), and unless new incomes are saved in full, markets for consumption goods will experience an increase in consumption demand. The resulting higher profitability in the late stages will attract resources back into consumer goods production. Because the economy does not have enough factors of production to simultaneously complete the newly initiated capital formations and meet the increased demand for consumption goods, some sectors must lose in this struggle for resources.

As shown earlier, the winning side is always the consumption stage. The early stages could continue their production only if the source of demand for their output did not dry up. In this case, the source comes from the released money balances. However, another round of the release is unlikely to occur. Compared to the quantity of money that can be created by monetary expansion, the amount of real money balances held by people is limited. The willingness to further reduce money balances may also be confined by the fact that greater demand for goods in the economy will increase prices, which, by definition, erodes real money balances. In other words, higher prices necessitate a larger share of assets to be held in the form of money, and the initial source of expansion will therefore dry up.

[10] Using a simple equation of exchange $MV = PY$, V increases instead of M. Further discussion appears in Potuzak (2016d, 2018, 2021) and Cochran and Call (1998, 2000).

The source of investment in the form of reduced money balances is therefore relatively mild, and the business cycle thus triggered would be quite moderate. Its magnitude critically depends on the interest-elasticity of the demand for money. The higher the sensitivity, the more money balances can be released. If the money demand were perfectly elastic, a situation known as the liquidity trap, the business cycle thus triggered could be considerable.

The entire process of the business cycle with an elastic money demand function is illustrated in the following system of diagrams. Figure 7.9 shows that a positive technological shock drives the natural interest rate up from $r_{nat,1}$ to $r_{nat,2}$. However, if the demand for money is sensitive to the interest rate, people can release part of their real money balances (ΔMd_r), and the market interest rate r_2 does not keep pace with the natural level ($r_2 < r_{nat,2}$). Part of the investment spending is not financed by the flow of saving ($I_2 > S$), because the demand for present consumer goods does not decline.

Figure 7.10 demonstrates that this reduction of money balances allows for a partial lengthening of the production structure by initiating roundabout methods. As shown in Fig. 7.11, sooner or later, the market interest rate will rise to the natural level ($r_3 = r_{nat,2}$), as the flow of money reaches consumers, and the demand for present consumption goods grows. The economy loses part of its capital, the creation of which began as a result of released money holdings. Figure 7.12 demonstrates that a higher interest rate cannot leave the structure of production unchanged. The eventual outcome is a partial destruction of capital in the economy and recession.

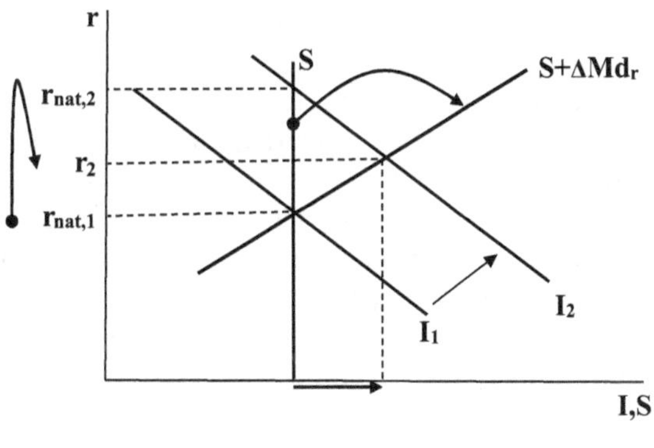

Fig. 7.9 A positive technological shock and a partial release of money balances

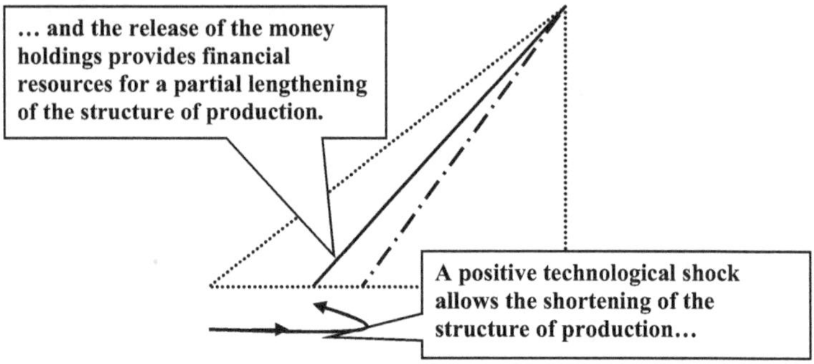

Fig. 7.10 A positive technological shock and a partial release of money balances

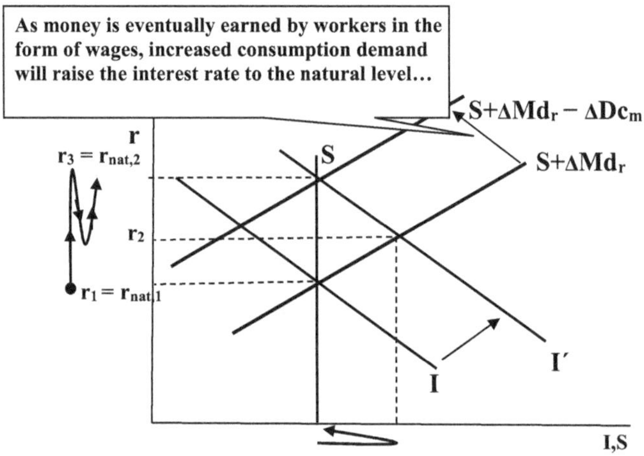

Fig. 7.11 Interest rate reversion

The prior analysis suggests that the business cycle may arise even under a fixed money supply. Austrian authors usually identify the elastic money supply as the cause of the boom-bust cycle. In their opinion, the elastic money supply is a necessary outcome of the central banking system and fractional reserves. The abolition of one or the other is therefore an essential condition for avoiding the business cycle. However, our analysis shows that, if the demand for money is highly sensitive to changes in the interest rate, business cycles can occur even in a world without a central bank.

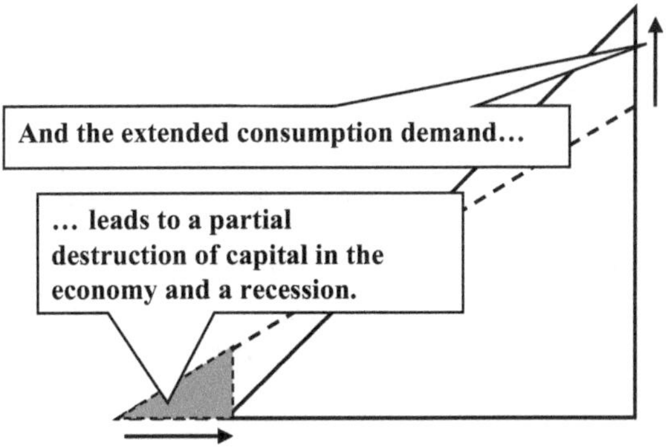

Fig. 7.12 Eventual recession in the Hayek triangle

References

Bagus, P. (2010). Austrian Business Cycle Theory: Are 100 Percent Reserves Sufficient to Prevent a Business Cycle? *Libertarian Papers, 2*(2), 1–18.

Bagus, P., & Howden, D. (2010). The Term Structure of Savings, the Yield Curve, and Maturity Mismatching. *The Quarterly Journal of Austrian Economics, 13*(3), 64–85.

Barnett, W., II, & Block, W. E. (2009). Crash and Carry: Financial Intermediaries, the Intertemporal-Carry Trade, and Austrian Business Cycles. *Ethics & Politics, XI*(1), 455–469.

Cassel, G. (1928). The Rate of Interest, the Bank Rate, and the Stabilization of Prices. *The Quarterly Journal of Economics, 42*(4), 511–529.

Cochran, J. P. (2004). Capital, Monetary Calculation, and the Trade Cycle: The Importance of Sound Money. *The Quarterly Journal of Austrian Economics, 7*(1), 17–25.

Cochran, J. P., & Call, S. P. (1998). Free Banking and Credit Creation: Implications for Business Cycle Theory. *The Quarterly Journal of Austrian Economics, 3*(3), 29–40.

Cochran, J. P., & Call, S. P. (2000). The Role of Fractional-Reserve Banking and Financial Intermediation in the Money Supply Process: Keynes and the Austrians. *The Quarterly Journal of Austrian Economics, 1*(3), 35–50.

Cochran, J. P., Call, S. P., & Glahe, F. R. (1999). Credit Creation or Financial Intermediation?: Fractional-Reserve Banking in a Growing Economy. *The Quarterly Journal of Austrian Economics, 2*(3), 53–64.

Cochran, J. P., Call, S. P., & Glahe, F. R. (2003). Austrian Business Cycle Theory: Variations on a Theme. *The Quarterly Journal of Austrian Economics, 6*(1), 67–73.

Fisher, I. (1930). *Theory of Interest*. The Macmillan Company.

von Hayek, F. A. (1933 [1929]). *Monetary Theory and the Trade Cycle.* Jonathan Cape.

von Hayek, F. A. (1941). *The Pure Theory of Capital.* The University of Chicago Press.

von Hayek, F. A. (1942). The Ricardo Effect. *Economica, 9*(34), 127–152.

Huerta de Soto, J. (2006 [1998]). *Money, Bank Credit, and Economic Cycles.* Ludwig von Mises Institute.

King, R. G., & Plosser, C. I. (1984). Money, Credit, and Prices in a Real Business Cycle. *The American Economic review, 74*(3), 363–380.

von Mises, L. (1996 [1949]). *Human Action: A Treatise on Economics* (4th ed.). Fox & Wilkes.

Potuzak, P. (2016a). Fisher and Mises on Zero Interest: A Reconsideration. *Prague Economic Papers, 25*(2), 202–220.

Potuzak, P. (2016b). *The Pure Time Preference Theory: A Neoclassical Critique.* Elsevier. Retrieved from SSRN: https://ssrn.com/abstract=2868789

Potuzak, P. (2016c). *What Can We Learn from the Böhm-Bawerkian Theory in the World of Zero Interest?* Elsevier. Retrieved from SSRN: https://ssrn.com/abstract=2865082

Potuzak P. (2016d) *Hayek MV-Rule.* Retrieved from SSRN: https://ssrn.com/abstract=2857719

Potuzak, P. (2018). Price Level Stabilization: Hayek contra Mainstream Economics. *Prague Economic Papers, 27*(4), 449–478.

Potuzak, P. (2021). Demand for Money and Hayekian Triangles. *Revista Procesos De Mercado, 18*(1), 299–317.

Rothbard, M. N. (2000 [1963]). *America's Great Depression.* Ludwig von Mises Institute.

Rothbard, M. N. (2004 [1962]). *Man, Economy, and State.* Ludwig von Mises Institute.

Selgin, G., & White, L. H. (1996). In Defense of Fiduciary Media—or, We Are not Devo(lutionists), We Are Misesians! *The Review of Austrian Economics, 9*, 83–107.

CHAPTER 8

The Natural Output and the Natural Rate of Interest

The Natural Output

Thus far, we have assumed that the economy fully used all of its resources. In modern terms, it operated at its potential, natural, full-employment level.[1] Hayek (1941) relaxed this assumption in his later works. His analysis begins in a state with abundant factors of production and consumption goods. However, our approach only partly follows his original reasoning, because it was developed for a positive technological shock and reduced money balances.

We explore the consequences of monetary expansion in an economy operating far below its potential level. The answer to the question of how it is possible that some resources are not fully utilized will be postponed. As shown, monetary expansion increases demand for production goods, which can only be met by transferring resources from other stages, specifically late stages close to final consumption. However, if the economy suffers from massive unemployment not only of labour but also of other complementary factors of production, especially in the form of circulating capital, new capital formations can be initiated without disrupting the continuous flow of goods to consumer markets. There is no need to

[1] In the New Keynesian literature, at least the first two cannot be used interchangeably (Mankiw & Romer, 1991a, 1991b).

P. Potuzak, *Austrian Theory of Capital and Business Cycle*,
https://doi.org/10.1007/978-3-031-18728-5_8

release resources from the stages that provide consumption goods at present or in the near future.[2]

There can be no doubt that absorbing previously idle factors of production can expand the total output of capital goods. In terms of the Austrian theory of capital, more roundabout methods of production can be initiated. The factors of production then earn incomes for their services in lengthening the production structure, that is, in expanding the supply of future consumption goods. These incomes are used primarily to purchase present consumption goods. We assume that there are many unsold consumption goods in the stocks of firms. As a result, higher demand can be met without pressing producers in late stages to increase their output. At this moment, the greater demand of more workers for more consumption goods is fully satisfied by the available supply.

Sooner or later, as new incomes are earned in all stages and demand increases, stocks of previously unsold consumer goods become depleted. At the same time, higher demand for consumption goods may be transmitted to the earliest stages, which leads to further lengthening of the production structure. As a result, a new need for resources will be felt at all stages. If some factors of production are still unemployed, they may be absorbed not only in the processes that create new capital goods, but also in the final consumption stages. At this moment, it is reasonable to assume that the flow of consumer goods is not as robust as before, especially if monetary expansion channels new funds to the early stages, where new capital goods are formed and where a majority of previously idle factors of production are employed. There must be a critical time when a larger number of workers, who were initially unemployed, face a more or less constant supply of consumer goods.

It should be emphasized that the newly initiated methods of capital formation will provide consumer goods only after a certain period of time, and this process cannot be accelerated. In contrast, demand for present consumption goods is boosted by new incomes earned by previously unemployed workers.

It is perfectly conceivable that continued monetary expansion will eventually reduce unemployment to its natural level, and full employment will be achieved. This constitutes the moment when the structure of production is lengthened to its maximum, because there are no other unused

[2] An economy below its production possibilities frontier (PPF) is also analysed by Ravier (2011).

resources available. At this point, the economy reaches its potential level. At first glance, monetary expansion seems to have eliminated unemployment and saved the economy from recession.

The crucial question is whether the allocation of labour and other resources caused by monetary expansion is sustainable. The newly initiated capital formations and the resulting production structure must be built in such a way that they are also maintained by the inflow of resources in the future. In other words, the system of demands and supplies and the consequent price structure that results from monetary expansion must be consistent with the state that prevails when money injection ceases. As a result, the flow of production goods (i.e. future consumption goods) at each stage of the production process must be consistent with the flow of demand for these goods in the form of voluntary saving, even without the life support provided by the central bank.

However, it is very likely that monetary expansion will not set up this ideal match. The new money was predominantly channelled to the early stages, where the production apparatus expanded. In contrast, the demand, which is fuelled by incomes generated in the early stages, is directed mainly at markets for present consumption goods. Thus, there is a mismatch, rather than a match, between supply and demand for present and future consumer goods.

Because the production process takes place over time, the newly initiated roundabout methods require additional resources in the future to be completed. Only fully completed processes can provide final consumption goods. However, once full employment is achieved in the economy, the early stages can only obtain the necessary resources at the expense of the later stages, that is, at the expense of the production of final consumption goods. As shown before, factors of production, such as labour, can only be attracted to the early stages by additional rounds of money expansion. If this happens, a given number of workers must be satisfied with a lesser amount of consumption goods.

This can be termed phase three of the process described in this section, which examines monetary expansion in an economy that begins below its potential level. Phase one is characterized by massive unemployment of workers and an abundance of consumer goods, so that newly employed workers can buy unsold consumption goods released from the stocks of firms. In the second phase, unemployment is further reduced, while stocks of consumer goods are gradually depleted. In the third phase, full employment is achieved, and workers are reallocated to the early stages due to continued monetary expansion. In this phase, we arrive at a well-known picture of an economy that produces more future consumption goods than is justified by voluntary saving, while consumers demand present consumption goods or goods that mature in the near future.

As analysed in preceding chapters, unless monetary expansion accelerates, resources must eventually be attracted back to stages that are closer to final consumption. Paradoxically, the economy would require more factors of production than the society is endowed with to maintain an artificially lengthened structure of production. At the same time, a large part of the incomes of these factors of production should be used to purchase future goods rather than present goods, otherwise new resources will be required to keep pace with increased consumption demand.

It is an indisputable fact that monetary expansion has the capacity to fully employ all resources in the economy. However, the resulting allocation of resources cannot be sustained and the newly created capital structures collapse. Many projects in the early stages of production will be abandoned because there are not enough resources to complete them, as all kinds of factors of production are in greater demand in the stages closer to final consumption.

Along with this abandonment of capital, workers are released onto the labour market. It would be naive to assume that they will be immediately absorbed in the late stages of production. The economy loses large amounts of capital, which results in a sharp decline in labour productivity. These workers are thus employable only at very low real wages, or they may be completely unemployable.

Massive unemployment eventually causes depressed demand for final consumption goods, leading to excessive accumulation of the goods in firms' inventories. As a result, the recession spreads and affects all stages of production. Interestingly, the economy can make full use of its resources, but if the allocation induced by monetary expansion is not in line with the (inter-temporal) preferences of consumers, this situation ends up with widespread unemployment of these resources. As shown earlier, the unsustainability of "potential" output arises from the fact that there are not enough resources to sustain the lengthened production structure unless people suddenly change their preferences in favour of future consumption goods.

Other points also deserve some attention. The final recessionary state of the economy is very similar to the one we started with—massive unemployment of resources of various kinds, unsold stocks of consumer goods, and so forth. Yet, monetary expansion does not seem to be the best tool to get these resources fully employed again. At the same time, a large part of the capital stock is lost, so potential output itself is certainly reduced in a recession. This observation is consistent with studies on potential output after the financial crisis of 2007–2008.[3]

Clearly, monetary expansion can push the economy to its potential level, but given the general misallocation of resources, this situation is not sustainable. The economy will end up at a lower level of potential output than before the monetary expansion, due to the partial destruction of capital. Moreover, it would be naive to assume that the banking system is unaffected by this process of capital abandonment. It is very likely that bank balance sheets will be disrupted by the overall collapse in the values of various collateral. However, the second-round effects of capital destruction are not the focus of our investigation here.

The final state of the economy is depicted in Fig. 8.1. Figure 6.9 in Chap. 6 illustrates the short-run impact of monetary expansion in the textbook IS-LM model. The market real interest rate falls below its natural level and real output rises above its potential level. In the long run, both real variables return to their natural levels. In Fig. 8.1, the losses in capital structures described earlier are reflected in the leftward shift in potential output Y^*. The graph also assumes a decline in the IS curve caused by the

Fig. 8.1 Eventual recession in the IS-LM model

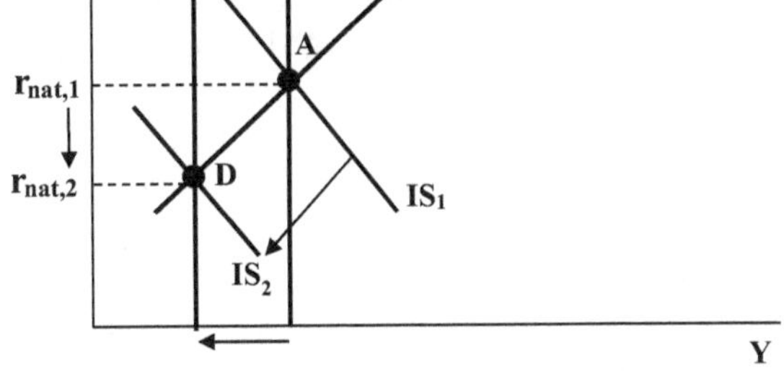

[3] See, for example, Furceri and Mourougane (2009).

disruption in the investment process. Shocks to the money supply can therefore leave permanent scars on the economy due to misallocation of resources. Money is not neutral in Austrian business cycle theory, because nominal shocks can affect the natural level of key real variables.

As the next section shows, the natural interest rate is likely to fall in recessions. The LM curve is also certainly affected, due to a partial collapse in deposits and money supply in recessions, which will shift the LM curve to the left. This creates further pressures in the form of "secondary" deflation.

The Natural Rate of Interest

The final issue to examine is the evolution of the natural rate of interest over the business cycle, illustrated in Fig. 6.2 in Chap. 6. As the prior analysis suggests, the natural rate of interest is likely to rise during economic booms, especially if the boom itself was initiated by a positive technological shock. However, if the central bank (or the entire banking system) does not follow the natural rate of interest, and the increase in the market interest rate is therefore delayed, economic growth is spurred by additional monetary and credit expansion. Powerful economic forces are triggered that eventually reverse the economic expansion, because the money-induced part of the economic boom is not sustainable.

Model results indicate that the market interest rate tends to return to its natural level. More important, however, is the overall restructuring of the economy after the money-induced boom. This process is accompanied by a significant loss of capital structures and massive unemployment. It would be naive to insist that the natural rate of interest remains unchanged throughout this turbulent process. We now explore whether economic analysis can identify trends in the natural interest rate in this context.

Consider the behaviour of the market interest rate and price inflation since the recent global financial crisis (i.e. in the long period since 2008). Both appear puzzling in relation to the theory developed here. Interest rates were depressed to zero for a very long time, and inflation rates were negligible. However, Austrian business cycle theory would predict that the economy should have suffered galloping inflation, because market interest rates were so low.

One possible explanation is that the natural rate of interest was also close to zero. Austrian theory predicts accelerating inflation not when the interest rate is low, but if the gap between the market interest rate and its natural counterpart is sufficiently negative. However, if there is no such gap, no inflation will arise. Because we observed very low inflation rates even in an environment of negligible interest rates, we can conclude that the natural rate of interest was also close to zero.[4]

Consider whether the Austrian model can explain why the natural rate of interest falls to such a low level in a recession. Indeed, some solutions can be found in the model. One is evident on the supply side of the loanable funds market, and another on the demand side. The very low natural rate of interest suggests that time preferences of people are insignificant. It is rather difficult to identify any reason why, in times of recession, people should value present goods only as much or even less than future goods. However, a theory developed by Fisher (1930) can offer some insights.

If people expect the time shape of their income stream to be stable or even to decline during a recession, their time preference may decrease. However, the permanent income hypothesis suggests that recessions are mainly associated with a decline in transitory, rather than in permanent, income. People should therefore expect their income to grow in the foreseeable future. From this perspective, in a recession when incomes are relatively low, people should reduce saving to smooth the flow of their consumption. Interest rates should therefore rise rather than fall. A downward trend in the interest rate occurs only if people expect the recession to be longer or if they expect it to deepen. These scenarios would result in a decreasing time shape of expected income. The first Böhm-Bawerkian cause of the interest rate would operate with the opposite sign (Potuzak, 2016a, 2016b, 2016c).

The second reason for the decline in time preference is closely related to the first. Recessions usually increase uncertainty about the path of future income. As a result, people may build up precautionary savings (Carroll, 1997), causing market interest rates to fall. In contrast, an economic downturn is associated with lower incomes. Fisher (1930) suggested that time preference can be negatively related to income levels. With lower income, time preference may increase, leading to a rise in the interest rate.

[4] Authors who studied optimal monetary policy when the nominal interest rate reached the zero lower bound explicitly assumed that the natural rate of interest could even be negative (Eggertsson & Woodford, 2003). This possibility is comprehensively explored in Potuzak (2016a, 2016b, 2016c).

In times of recession, people restructure their portfolios and buy safer assets at the expense of riskier ones. As a result, interest rates fall for the former and rise for the latter. The interest rate in the model is a theoretical concept, so it is difficult to choose the most representative rate from the real world. The spread between safe and risky interest rates can widen in a recession, making this choice even harder. If we select a safe interest rate, it is likely to decline in periods with a higher risk premium, and a recession can be a good example of such a situation.

This brings us to another important fact. It is conceivable that the market rate of interest is well above zero, even if the central bank sets its interest rate close to zero. This type of monetary policy is merely a measure to heal the balance sheets of commercial banks that have been adversely affected by the recession. In other words, by borrowing money from the central bank at an interest rate close to zero and lending it at a much higher market interest rate, commercial banks can improve their profitability and stability. In addition, commercial banks may be reluctant to lend money if the overall value of collateral in the economy declines. At the same time, the overall demand for credit during a recession is not very high, so that no significant amounts of money will ultimately be injected into the real economy.

The last sentence of the previous paragraph mentioned the second blade of the loanable funds market, that is, the demand for loanable funds. Because recessions are usually associated with serious losses of physical capital, the willingness of firms to expand their capital stock is frozen. Because investment spending represents a flow into capital stock, it can be significantly reduced when the demand for capital falls. We can identify many reasons why the investment curve in the loanable funds market is depressed in a recession. Weak investment demand can, in turn, decrease the natural rate of interest to very low levels.

Thus far, we have identified various reasons for a very low natural rate of interest, which may come from either the supply or the demand side of the loanable funds market. Finally, we can imagine a situation in which the loanable funds market is completely unaffected by changes in monetary policy. This situation is the famous liquidity trap presented by Keynes (1936). If the demand for money is infinitely elastic, which can occur at very low nominal interest rates, massive injections of money supply are completely absorbed into the money balances of individuals and are not offered as loans to firms. The supply curve in the loanable funds market does not shift to the right, because the increase in the money supply, which pushes the curve to the right, is offset by a one-to-one increase in the demand for money, moving this curve back.

The inability of the central bank to follow the natural rate of interest can trigger a business cycle. Over the course of the business cycle, the structure of production can become so disorganized that the eventual level of the natural interest rate remains hidden. This can pose a serious problem for the central bank in its conduct of practical monetary policy, and raises the question of whether the interest rate is the best policy instrument. This section indicates that the answer may not be in the affirmative.

References

Carroll, C. D. (1997). Buffer-Stock Saving and the Life Cycle/Permanent Income Hypothesis. *The Quarterly Journal of Economics, 112*(1), 1–55.

Eggertsson, G. B., & Woodford, M. (2003). The Zero Bound on Interest Rates and Optimal Monetary Policy. *Brookings Papers on Economic Activity, 1*, 139–211.

Fisher, I. (1930). *Theory of Interest*. The Macmillan Company.

Furceri, D., & Mourougane, A. (2009). *The Effect of Financial Crises on Potential Output: New Empirical Evidence from OECD Countries*. OECD Economics Department. Working Papers 699.

von Hayek, F. A. (1941). *The Pure Theory of Capital*. The University of Chicago Press.

Keynes, J. M. (1936). *The General Theory of Employment, Interest and Money*. Harcourt, Brace, and Company.

Mankiw, N. G., & Romer, D. (Eds.). (1991a). *New Keynesian Economics: Volume 1*. MIT Press.

Mankiw, N. G., & Romer, D. (Eds.). (1991b). *New Keynesian Economics: Volume 2*. MIT Press.

Potuzak, P. (2016a). Fisher and Mises on Zero Interest: A Reconsideration. *Prague Economic Papers, 25*(2), 202–220.

Potuzak, P. (2016b). *The Pure Time Preference Theory: A Neoclassical Critique*. Elsevier. Retrieved from SSRN: https://ssrn.com/abstract=2868789

Potuzak, P. (2016c). *What Can We Learn from the Böhm-Bawerkian Theory in the World of Zero Interest?* Elsevier. Retrieved from SSRN: https://ssrn.com/abstract=2865082

Ravier, A. O. (2011). Rethinking Capital Based Macroeconomics. *The Quarterly Journal of Austrian Economics, 14*(3), 347–375.

CHAPTER 9

Conclusion

The core of the Austrian theories of capital and the business cycle is the allocation of factors of production over time, which can be either sustainable or unsustainable. Sustainable allocation is associated with real economic growth that can be driven by lower time preference in the society, or by technological progress. Unsustainable allocation is caused by monetary forces coming either from the central bank and commercial banks on the supply side or from changing liquidity preference on the demand side. The initial dynamics of sustainable and unsustainable paths are very similar. However, money-induced economic booms end in misallocation of resources and painful recessions. This book develops a graphical apparatus that separates these two cases. This approach can complement traditional textual explanations of Austrian theory, as well as the standard Hayek triangles.

Part I of this book identifies time as a key element in Austrian capital theory. We demonstrate that capital cannot be considered a homogeneous mass without a structure that is automatically maintained. These properties are illustrated in a transition process from a shorter to a longer production method as time preferences decline. The new diagrammatical apparatus shows the nature of saving and investment in this process. New forms of capital are created as a result of reallocation of factors of production. Output of present consumption goods temporarily drops, but the new technique eventually produces a greater quantity of goods. The analysis shows that a higher growth rate of the consumer goods output cannot

P. Potuzak, *Austrian Theory of Capital and Business Cycle*,
https://doi.org/10.1007/978-3-031-18728-5_9

be sustained if roundabout methods exhibit diminishing marginal productivity. In this respect, our approach corrects mistakes made by some Austrian scholars.

Part II focuses on Austrian business cycle theory. A similar set of tools is applied to show that intertemporal allocation of resources can be disturbed by a monetary shock. This chapter examines the U-shaped evolution of the interest rate over the business cycle. It defends Austrian theory against its critics. The key argument is that an increase in the interest rate at the beginning of the downswing phase of the business cycle is caused by a drop in real saving, which has its genetic code in the boom phase. This chapter also applies Hayek triangles to map economic fluctuations caused by a real shock, which is accommodated by the banking system. Specifically, an unsustainable boom can be caused not only by an active banking system, but also by passive behaviour of banks that do not raise the market interest rate sufficiently when a positive technological shock increases the natural rate of interest. The same apparatus elucidates the consequences of sensitive demand for money, which has been overlooked in prior Austrian literature.

The Austrian model suggests that the natural rate of interest and potential output can be affected by the business cycle process. Therefore, money can be non-neutral in the long run. The analysis in this book also suggests that changes in capital productivity can significantly affect the natural rate of interest, which is not consistent with the pure time preference theory advocated by Mises and Rothbard. A deeper discussion of time preference and its relationship to the natural interest rate is intentionally omitted here, but we refer the interested reader to other works. [1]

Another straightforward extension of Austrian theory is business cycle analysis in a growing economy. Hayek suggested that the general price level should be decreasing in an economy with expanding potential output. Stabilizing the price level in a growing economy requires monetary expansion, which can be a source of business cycles. From this perspective, inflation targeting is not an optimal monetary policy regime. This opens a new space in the search for a better monetary policy framework.[2]

Neoclassical theory emphasizes the dynamic nature of economic models. However, mainstream economics neglects important issues in the

[1] See, for example, Potuzak (2016a, 2016b, 2016c).

[2] The underlying theory and alternative rules are presented in Potuzak (2016d, 2017, 2018).

theory of capital. In contrast, Austrian capital theory lacks the sophisticated mathematical apparatus of modern growth theory. Natural evolution may be a way to integrate these two theories into one comprehensive model. Such cooperation can also help us to understand unsettled issues in business cycle theory, which usually overlooks the importance of capital allocation in the short run.

In my opinion, the knowledge problem introduced by Hayek (1937, 1945) is crucial in business cycle theory. Because the real and monetary parts of the economy are interrelated, the central bank's response to events in the real economy can never leave the real variables, on which the central bank based its action, unaffected. As a result, conducting monetary policy in good faith may cause more damage than anyone imagined before taking an action. Our understanding of the complex processes of the economy is rather limited. The institutional framework in which central banks operate seems to give them too much power and discretion. This framework is based on the idea that our knowledge has advanced to a point where the economy can be fine-tuned without significant risk of failure.

References

Potuzak, P. (2016a). Fisher and Mises on Zero Interest: A Reconsideration. *Prague Economic Papers, 25*(2), 202–220.

Potuzak, P. (2016b). *The Pure Time Preference Theory: A Neoclassical Critique*. Elsevier. Retrieved from SSRN: https://ssrn.com/abstract=2868789

Potuzak, P. (2016c). *What Can We Learn from the Böhm-Bawerkian Theory in the World of Zero Interest?* Retrieved from SSRN: https://ssrn.com/abstract=2865082

Potuzak P. (2016d) *Hayek MV-Rule*. Retrieved from SSRN: https://ssrn.com/abstract=2857719

Potuzak, P. (2017). *The Hayek-Taylor Rule*. Retrieved from SSRN: https://ssrn.com/abstract=2972121

Potuzak, P. (2018). Price Level Stabilization: Hayek Contra Mainstream Economics. *Prague Economic Papers, 27*(4), 449–478.

von Hayek, F. A. (1937). Economics and Knowledge. *Economica, 4*(*13*), 33–54.

von Hayek, F. A. (1945). The Use of Knowledge in Society. *The American Economic Review, 35*(4), 519–530.

Author Index[1]

B

C

F

H

J

K

[1] Note: Page numbers followed by 'n' refer to notes.

P. Potuzak, *Austrian Theory of Capital and Business Cycle*,
https://doi.org/10.1007/978-3-031-18728-5

Subject Index[1]

[1] Note: Page numbers followed by 'n' refer to notes.

P. Potuzak, *Austrian Theory of Capital and Business Cycle*,
https://doi.org/10.1007/978-3-031-18728-5

FSC
www.fsc.org
MIX
Papier | Fördert
gute Waldnutzung
FSC® C083411

Kolibri 360 GmbH
Ferdinand-Jühlke-Straße 7
99095 Erfurt, Deutschland
produktsicherheit@kolibri360.de